Intermediate 2

Biology

2004 Exam

2005 Exam

2006 Exam

2007 Exam

2008 Exam

Leckie × Leckie

© Scottish Qualifications Authority
All rights reserved. Copying prohibited. No part of this publication may be reproduced, stored in a retrieval system, or transmitted
in any form or by any means, electronic, mechanical, photocopying, recording or otherwise.

First exam published in 2004.
Published by Leckie & Leckie Ltd, 3rd Floor, 4 Queen Street, Edinburgh EH2 1JE
tel: 0131 220 6831 fax: 0131 225 9987 enquiries@leckieandleckie.co.uk www.leckieandleckie.co.uk

ISBN 978-1-84372-656-2

A CIP Catalogue record for this book is available from the British Library.

Leckie & Leckie is a division of Huveaux plc.

Leckie & Leckie is grateful to the copyright holders, as credited at the back of the book, for permission to use their material.
Every effort has been made to trace the copyright holders and to obtain their permission for the use of copyright material.
Leckie & Leckie will gladly receive information enabling them to rectify any error or omission in subsequent editions.

[BLANK PAGE]

FOR OFFICIAL USE

Total for
Sections B and C

X007/201

NATIONAL
QUALIFICATIONS
2004

WEDNESDAY, 19 MAY
9.00 AM – 11.00 AM

BIOLOGY
INTERMEDIATE 2

Fill in these boxes and read what is printed below.

Full name of centre

Oldmachar Academy

Town

Aberdeen

Forename(s)

Sophie

Surname

Murray

Date of birth
Day Month Year

0 6 0 1 9 3

Scottish candidate number

0 3 0 3 2 1 6 7 3

Number of seat

SECTION A (25 marks)

Instructions for completion of Section A are given on page two.

SECTIONS B AND C (75 marks)

1 (a) All questions should be attempted.

(b) It should be noted that in **Section C** questions 1 and 2 each contain a choice.

2 The questions may be answered in any order but all answers are to be written in the spaces provided in this answer book, and must be written clearly and legibly in ink.

3 Additional space for answers and rough work will be found at the end of the book. If further space is required, supplementary sheets may be obtained from the invigilator and should be inserted inside the **front** cover of this book.

4 The numbers of questions must be clearly inserted with any answers written in the additional space.

5 Rough work, if any should be necessary, should be written in this book and then scored through when the fair copy has been written.

6 Before leaving the examination room you must give this book to the invigilator. If you do not, you may lose all the marks for this paper.

SCOTTISH
QUALIFICATIONS
AUTHORITY

©

Read carefully

1 Check that the answer sheet provided is for Biology Intermediate 2 (Section A).

2 Fill in the details required on the answer sheet.

3 In this section a question is answered by indicating the choice A, B, C or D by a stroke made in **ink** in the appropriate place in the answer sheet—see the sample question below.

4 For each question there is only **one** correct answer.

5 Rough working, if required, should be done only on this question paper, or on the rough working sheet provided—**not** on the answer sheet.

6 At the end of the examination the answer sheet for Section A **must** be placed inside the front cover of this answer book.

Sample Question

Which part of the brain is involved in the control of heart rate?

A Cerebellum

B Medulla

C Hypothalamus

D Cerebrum

The correct answer is B—Medulla. A **heavy** vertical line should be drawn joining the two dots in the appropriate box in the column headed **B** as shown **in the example on the answer sheet**.

If, after you have recorded your answer, you decide that you have made an error and wish to make a change, you should cancel the original answer and put a vertical stroke in the box you now consider to be correct. Thus, if you want to change an answer **D** to an answer **B**, your answer sheet would look like this:

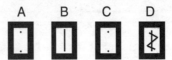

If you want to change back to an answer which has already been scored out, you should **enter a tick (✓)** to the RIGHT of the box of your choice, thus:

SECTION A

All questions in this Section should be attempted.

1. The energy values of different food materials are shown in the table.

Food	Energy value (kJ per gram)
Glucose	4
Protein	4
Fat	9

How much energy is contained in a food sample consisting of 3 grams of glucose and 2 grams of fat?

A 17 kJ

B 21 kJ

C 30 kJ

D 35 kJ

2. The function of the villi is to increase the surface area for

A absorption

B protection

C acid production

D peristalsis.

3. Bile is stored in the

A liver

B gall bladder

C stomach

D small intestine.

4. A piece of carrot weighs 20 g fresh and 2 g dry. What is the percentage water content of the carrot?

A   2%

B 10%

C 72%

D 90%

5. The table below shows the rate of blood flow to the body at rest and during strenuous exercise.

Which line in the table shows the greatest increase in blood flow during strenuous exercise?

	Region of body	Blood flow (cm^3/minute)	
		at rest	strenuous exercise
A	brain	750	750
B	muscle	1200	22 000
C	heart	250	750
D	skin	500	600

Questions 6 and 7 refer to the diagram which shows the structure of the lungs.

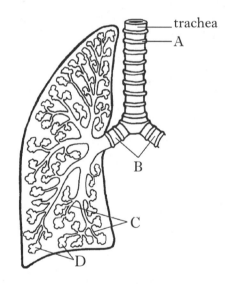

6. Which label identifies the bronchioles?

7. The function of part A is to

A prevent the lungs from collapsing

B keep the trachea open at all times

C prevent food entering the windpipe

D trap dirt and bacteria.

[Turn over

8. Which line in the table below identifies correctly how macrophages destroy bacteria?

	Phagocytosis	Antibody production
A	yes	yes
(B)	yes	no
C	no	yes
D	no	no

9. The diagram below represents a unicellular organism.

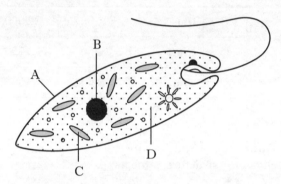

Which part indicates this is a plant cell?

C

10. The diagram below shows onion cells as observed under a microscope at a magnification of 100 X.

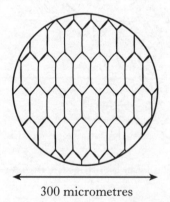

300 micrometres

The diameter of the field of view is 300 micrometres. The average width of each cell in micrometres is

(A) 0·38

B 0·75

C 37·5

D 75·0.

11. Which line in the table below correctly matches the organism, product and the commercial use of the product?

	Organism	Product	Commercial use of product
A	yeast	methane	biogas
B	bacteria	alcohol	biogas
(C)	yeast	alcohol	gasohol
D	bacteria	methane	gasohol

12. The graph below shows the effect of increasing antibiotic concentrations on the percentage of bacteria surviving within a population. None of the bacteria had resistance to the antibiotic.

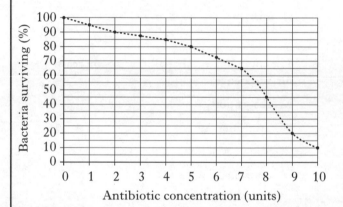

Another experiment was carried out with different bacteria, some of which had resistance to the antibiotic.

Which of the following **best** describes the effect on the bacteria surviving in this second experiment?

A The percentage of bacteria surviving would increase.

(B) The percentage of bacteria surviving would decrease.

C There would be no change in the percentage of bacteria surviving.

D All of the bacteria would survive.

13. Two grams of fresh liver was added to hydrogen peroxide.

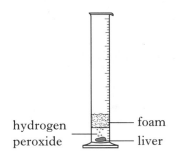

hydrogen peroxide — foam
— liver

The time taken to collect $10 \, cm^3$ of oxygen foam was 2 minutes.

The rate of oxygen production was

A $2 \cdot 5 \, cm^3/g/min$

B $5 \cdot 0 \, cm^3/g/min$

C $10 \cdot 0 \, cm^3/g/min$

D $20 \cdot 0 \, cm^3/g/min$.

14. The diagram below illustrates an investigation of respiration in yeast.

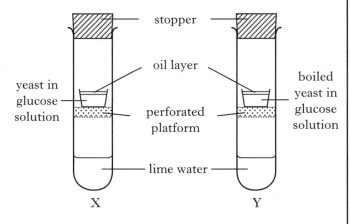

stopper

oil layer

yeast in glucose solution

perforated platform

boiled yeast in glucose solution

lime water

X   Y

Lime water is an indicator which changes from clear to cloudy in the presence of carbon dioxide.

The investigation was allowed to run for 24 hours.

Which line in the table below identifies correctly the appearance of the lime water in tubes X and Y after 24 hours?

	X	Y
A	clear	clear
B	cloudy	cloudy
C	clear	cloudy
D	cloudy	clear

15. Which of the following are **all** limiting factors in photosynthesis?

A   Carbon dioxide concentration, temperature and light intensity

B   Carbon dioxide concentration, oxygen concentration and light intensity

C   Oxygen concentration, temperature and light intensity

D   Oxygen concentration, carbon dioxide concentration and temperature

16. Which line in the table below identifies the **best** conditions for the production of early crops?

	Added factor	Light intensity
A	oxygen	high
B	oxygen	medium
C	carbon dioxide	medium
D	carbon dioxide	high

17. The following stages occur during photosynthesis.

W   glucose is formed
X   water is broken down to produce hydrogen
Y   glucose is converted to starch
Z   hydrogen is combined with carbon dioxide

The correct order for these stages is

A   W Z X Y

B   Z Y X W

C   X Z W Y

D   Y X Z W.

18. Which of the following is a correct description of a decomposer?

A   A micro-organism which lives inside animals and causes disease.

B   An organism which releases chemicals from organic waste.

C   A fungus which grows on living tissue.

D   A green plant which roots in rotting vegetation.

[Turn over

19. The following diagram shows a pyramid of energy. Which level is the result of the energy from the sun being converted into chemical energy?

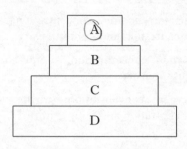

20. The following choice chamber was used to investigate the effect of humidity on the behaviour of woodlice.

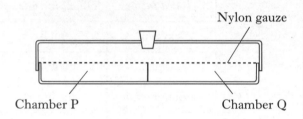

Nylon gauze

Chamber P   Chamber Q

Which line in the table below describes the **best** experimental set up?

	Number of woodlice	Contents of chamber P	Contents of chamber Q	Modification to choice chamber
A	10	Drying agent	Wet cotton wool	Half covered in black paper
B	10	Wet cotton wool	Drying agent	Totally covered in black paper
C	20	Drying agent	Wet cotton wool	Half covered in black paper
D	20	Wet cotton wool	Drying agent	Totally covered in black paper

21. The diagram below shows the main parts of a flower.

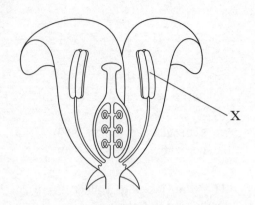

X

Which line in the table identifies X and the type of gamete it produces?

	Name of X	Type of gamete produced
A	ovary	male
B	ovary	female
C	anther	female
D	anther	male

22. The information below refers to some woodland birds.

Bird species	Common food eaten	Nest location
Lesser spotted woodpecker	insects	dead trees
Green woodpecker	ants, other insects	live trees
Greater spotted woodpecker	insects, nuts, seeds	live trees
Treecreeper	insects, spiders, seeds	dead trees

Between which two bird species will competition for food and nest location be greatest?

A   Lesser spotted woodpecker and treecreeper

B   Greater spotted woodpecker and lesser spotted woodpecker

C   Lesser spotted woodpecker and green woodpecker

D   Greater spotted woodpecker and treecreeper

23. In humans, all sperm contain

    A   an X chromosome

    B   a Y chromosome

    C   an X and Y chromosome

    (D) either an X or a Y chromosome.

24. The graph below shows the average number of peppered moths, in a woodland, in June of each year over a 10 year period.

Key   ----•-- light form

   ——■— dark form

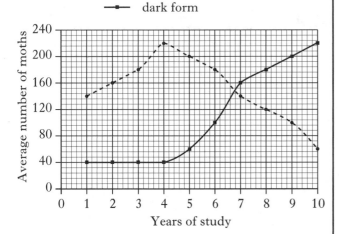

Years of study

Studies have shown that an increase in the number of dark moths is related to an increase in the level of pollution in the atmosphere.

Which of the following **best** describes what would happen to the number of moths if measures were introduced to reduce air pollution from year 7?

(A) Increase in dark moths and decrease in light moths

B   Decrease in dark moths and increase in light moths

C   Increase in dark moths and increase in light moths

D   Decrease in dark moths and decrease in light moths

25. Genetic engineering can be used to alter bacterial cells in order to produce human insulin.

The following stages occur during genetic engineering.

1   Insulin gene extracted from a human cell

2   Bacteria divide and produce large quantities of human insulin

3   Plasmid is removed from bacterial cell and "cut" open

4   Insulin gene is inserted into bacterial plasmid

The correct sequence of these stages is

(A) 1 3 4 2

B   1 3 2 4

C   3 4 2 1

D   3 1 2 4.

Candidates are reminded that the answer sheet for Section A MUST be placed INSIDE the front cover of this answer book.

[Turn over for Section B on *Page eight*

SECTION B

Marks

All questions in this section should be attempted.

1. An experiment was set up to investigate the effect of pH on the action of the enzyme salivary amylase.

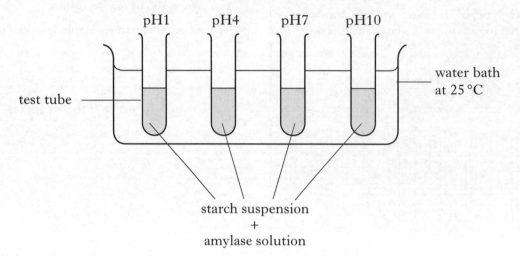

After 30 minutes a sample from each test tube was tested for the presence of simple sugars.

(a)   (i)   Other than temperature, state **two** variables that must be kept constant in the experiment.

1   the time (30 minutes) of the experiment

2   the concentration of amylase solution   ②

(ii)   Name the reagent used to test for simple sugars.

Benedicts solution   ①

(b)   The results obtained are shown in the table below.

pH	Simple sugars test
1	negative
4	negative
7	positive
10	negative

Marks

1. **(*b*)** **(continued)**

    (i) What conclusion can be drawn from these results?

        Simple sugars are only present in a neutral pH level.

        ①

    (ii) Predict the results if the enzyme had been boiled before use. Give an explanation for your answer.

        Prediction   no results

        Explanation the extreme heat would've caused the enzyme to become denatured

        ②

(*c*) Explain why food containing starch must be digested before it can be used in the human body.

    The starch molecules need to be broken down and seperated so the molecules can be absorbed better. Glucose?

    ②

[Turn over

Marks

2. (*a*) Complete the following sentences by <u>underlining</u> **one** option in each pair of brackets to describe correctly the body's response to exposure to **low** temperature.

The temperature change is detected by receptors in the skin which send nerve impulses to the $\left\{ \begin{array}{c} \underline{\text{hypothalamus}} \\ \text{pituitary} \end{array} \right\}$. Nerve impulses are then sent to arterioles in the skin causing them to $\left\{ \begin{array}{c} \underline{\text{constrict}} \\ \text{dilate} \end{array} \right\}$. Sweat production $\left\{ \begin{array}{c} \underline{\text{decreases}} \\ \text{increases} \end{array} \right\}$ to help return the body temperature to normal.

②

(*b*) The table below lists the stages in a reflex arc. Each stage is represented by a letter.

Stage	Letter
An impulse passes through a motor neurone	A
An impulse passes through a sensory neurone	B
The effector brings about a response	C
A receptor detects a stimulus	D
An impulse passes through a relay neurone	E

(i) Complete the following flow chart to show the correct order of these stages.

The first stage has been given.

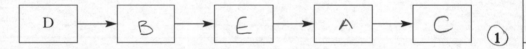

①

(ii) What is the function of reflex actions?

<u>To protect.</u>

①

Marks

3. The diagram shows part of the digestive system.

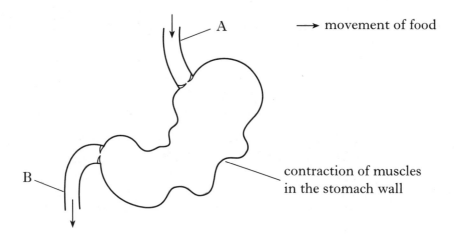

A

→ movement of food

B

contraction of muscles
in the stomach wall

(a) Name structures A and B.

A _oesophagus_

B _small intestine_   ②

(b) Name **one** type of muscle found in the stomach wall.

Longitudinal   ①

(c) How do the contractions of the muscles in the stomach wall help the digestion of food?

They help the food move along.   1

[Turn over

Marks

4. The oxygen concentration of the air decreases as the height above sea level increases.

   The table below shows the red blood cell count of a mountaineer taken at different heights above sea level.

Height above sea level (metres)	Red blood cell count (millions/mm^3 of blood)
200	5·0
1000	5·6
2200	6·5
3600	7·6
4800	8·5

   (a) On the grid, plot a line graph to show red blood cell count against height above sea level.

   (Additional graph paper, if required, will be found on page 30.)

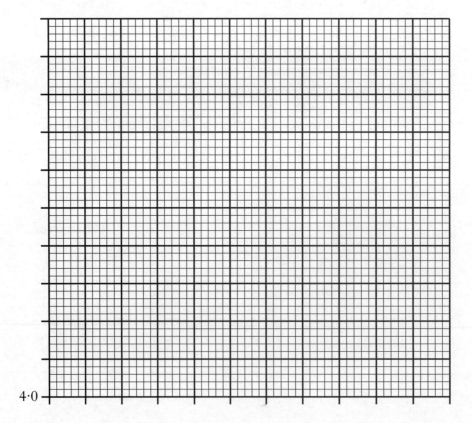

4·0

3

DO NOT WRITE IN THIS MARGIN

Marks

4. (continued)

(*b*) (i) From the table, describe the relationship between the height above sea level and the red blood cell count.

As the height above sea level increases, so does the red blood cell count. **1**

(ii) Explain the importance of this change in the red blood cell count.

It means the body is trying to oxygenate the body by producing more red blood cells. **1**

[Turn over

Marks

5. (a) The diagram below shows the unicellular organism *Paramecium* which lives in freshwater.

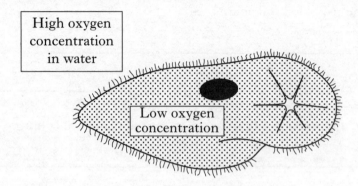

High oxygen concentration in water

Low oxygen concentration

   (i) Name the process by which oxygen moves from the water into the organism.

      Osmosis

   (ii) Name a substance that moves from the organism into the water.

      Glucose

   (iii) Name the cell structure which controls the entry and exit of materials.

      Cell membrane

Marks

5. **(continued)**

(*b*) The diagram below shows the internal structure of a leaf.

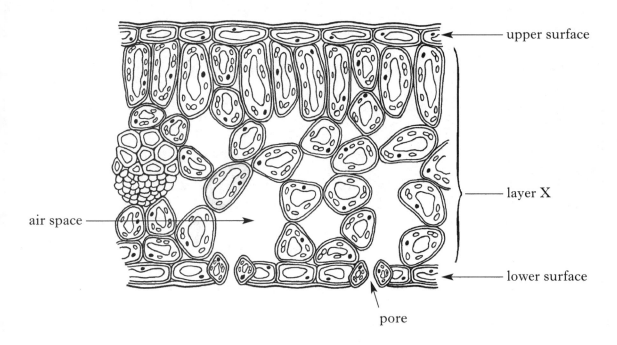

During the hours of daylight, the concentration of carbon dioxide in the air spaces is higher than in the cells of layer X.

Explain why this difference in concentration is important to the leaf cells.

The absence of carbon dioxide in the air spaces would mean there would be more oxygen and photosynthesis would fail lulz.

2

[Turn over

Marks

6. Four groups of students carried out an investigation into the effect of the micro-organisms present in live yoghurt on milk. The milk was first sterilised to remove all micro-organisms present. Each group set up 3 beakers as shown below.

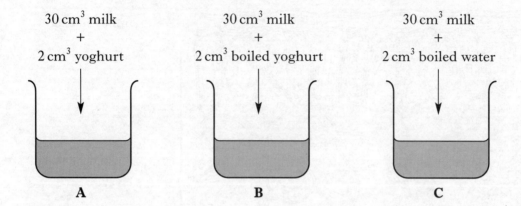

A lid was placed over each beaker. The beakers were placed in a water bath at 35 °C. The pH of the contents of each beaker was measured at the start and 6 hours later.

(a) (i) Name the type of micro-organism found in live yoghurt.

<u>Bacteria</u>   ①

(ii) Name the substance, produced by these micro-organisms, which causes a change in the pH of the milk.

<u>Yeast</u>   1

(iii) Suggest why the lid was placed over each beaker.

<u>To prevent airborne micro-organisms</u>
<u>from entering the beakers.</u>   ①

(iv) Why was beaker C included as a control?

<u>To see how milk reacted on it's own compared</u>
<u>to the other two.</u>   ①

Marks

6. (continued)

(*b*) The results from the 4 groups are given in the table below.

| Beaker | Change in pH | | | | |
	Group 1	Group 2	Group 3	Group 4	Average
A	−1·3	−1·8	−1·0	−1·5	−1·4
B	0·0	−1·2	0·0	0·0	−0·3
C	0·0	0·0	0·0	0·0	0·0

(i) Complete the table to show the average change in pH for beaker A.

Space for calculation

$$-1\cdot3$$
$$-1\cdot8$$
$$-1\cdot0$$
$$-1\cdot5$$
$$\overline{-5\cdot6}$$

$$4\overline{)5\cdot6} = 1\cdot4$$

① 1

(ii) Why were the results from the 4 groups collected and an average calculated?

To create a more reliable outcome.

① 1

(iii) Account for the unexpected result in beaker B of group 2.

The milk may have not been entirely sterilised.

① 1

[Turn over

DO NO
WRITE
THIS
MARGI

Marks

7. (*a*) An investigation into the effects of solutions of different salt concentrations on red blood cells was carried out. Three microscope slides were set up as shown below.

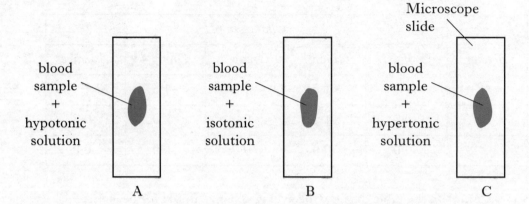

Microscope slide

blood sample + hypotonic solution A

blood sample + isotonic solution B

blood sample + hypertonic solution C

Each blood sample was observed under a microscope after 10 minutes.

(i) Describe what would have happened to the red blood cells on slides A and C.

Slide A _____

Slide C _____   1

(ii) Name the process responsible for these changes.

_____   1

(iii) What is meant by an **isotonic solution**?

_____

_____   1

(*b*) (i) State **one** osmoregulatory problem experienced by marine bony fish.

_____   1

(ii) Describe **one** method used by these fish to overcome the problem.

_____   1

Marks

8. The diagram below shows the main stages of aerobic respiration.

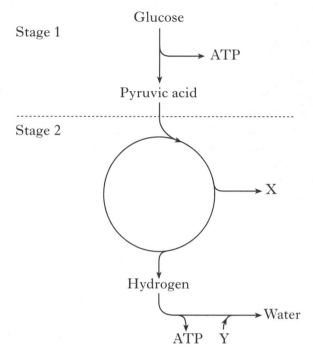

(a) Name Stage 1.

_____   1

(b) Name substances X and Y.

X _____

Y _____   1

(c) Which substance shown in the diagram is the **source** of the energy used to synthesise ATP?

_____   1

(d) Complete the following word equation which represents the synthesis of ATP.

_____ + _____ + energy ⟶ ATP   1

(e) How many molecules of ATP are produced per glucose molecule during each of the following stages?

Stage 1 _____

Stage 2 _____   2

(f) During aerobic respiration some energy is lost from the cell.
In what form is this energy?

_____   1

Marks

9. (*a*) A natural pine forest provides excellent habitats for many different organisms.

One of these organisms is a large bird called the capercaillie which nests in the deep vegetation on the forest floor. In summertime it eats berries, leaves and stems of the blaeberry and other forest plants. In winter it eats Scots pine needles and cones.

The capercaillie's natural predators are the fox and the wild cat. Crows eat their eggs.

Use information from the passage to answer the following questions.

(i) Complete the boxes below to show a food chain.

1

(ii) Complete the table of terms and named examples from the passage.

Term	Named example
ecosystem	
	all the crows
herbivore	

2

(iii) Natural pine forests show high biodiversity. What is meant by the term biodiversity?

_____

_____

1

DO NOT WRITE IN THIS MARGIN

Marks

9. (continued)

(*b*) The number of capercaillie in Scotland fell from 20 000 in 1970 to 3000 in 1991.

During the same period there was a large increase in the numbers of animals such as deer and sheep which graze on the forest floor.

Explain how this might have caused the decrease in the numbers of capercaillie.

____

____ **1**

(*c*) Give **one** example of a human activity which could affect biodiversity.

____ **1**

[Turn over

Marks

10. (a) In the fruitfly *Drosophila melanogaster*, the dominant form (G) of one gene determines grey body colour; black body colour results from the recessive form (g) of the gene.

The genotypes of the parent flies used in a cross are shown below.

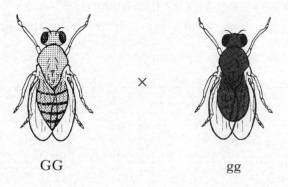

GG   ×   gg

(i) State the genotype(s) of the F_1 offspring of this cross.

_____

1

(ii) Decide if each of the following statements about this cross is **True** or **False**, and tick (✓) the appropriate box.

If the statement is **False**, write the correct word in the **Correction** box to replace the word underlined in the statement.

Statement	*True*	*False*	*Correction*
The different forms of the gene are <u>hybrids</u>.			
The <u>parents</u> in this cross are true breeding.			
The F_1 flies are <u>homozygous</u>.			

3

Marks

10. (a) (continued)

(iii) Two flies from the F_1 were allowed to breed together. This produced 56 grey flies and 14 black flies in the F_2.

Express this result as a simple whole number ratio.

Space for calculation

_____ grey flies : _____ black flies   1

(iv) The expected ratio of grey flies to black flies in the F_2 is 3:1. Suggest why the observed ratio was different from the expected ratio.

_____

_____   1

(b) In a study of variation, a group of students collected information on the heights and blood groups of a class.

For each variation state whether it is continuous or discontinuous.

Height _____

Blood groups _____   1

(c) Polygenic inheritance occurs as a result of the interaction of several genes. Give an example of polygenic inheritance in humans.

_____   1

[Turn over

Marks

11. (a) Complete the table to give the site of production and number of chromosomes of each type of gamete.

Human gamete	Site of production	Number of chromosomes
egg		
sperm		

2

(b) The diagram below shows the chromosome complement of a cell about to divide to form gametes.

   (i) How many sets of chromosomes does this cell contain?

   _____

1

   (ii) Name the type of cell division which produces gametes.

   _____

1

   (iii) The following diagram shows one way in which these chromosomes may line up during cell division.

   Complete the diagram below to show one other way in which the chromosomes may line up.

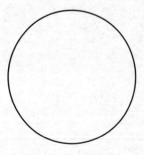

1

DO NOT WRITE IN THIS MARGIN

Marks

11. (continued)

(*c*) Chromosome pairs line up in a variety of ways.

Explain why this random assortment is important.

____

____ **1**

[Turn over for SECTION C on *Page twenty-six*

DO NO
WRITE
THIS
MARG

Marks

SECTION C

Both questions in this section should be attempted.

Note that each question contains a choice.

Questions 1 and 2 should be attempted on the blank pages which follow.

Supplementary sheets, if required, may be obtained from the invigilator.

1. Answer **either** A **or** B.

    A. The diagram below shows a section through the human heart.

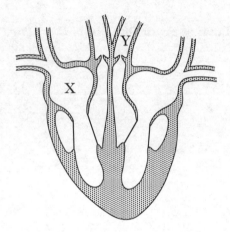

Describe the pathway of blood through the heart and associated structures starting at X and finishing at Y. There is no need to mention the valves.

5

   OR

    B. Urine production occurs in the kidney. The diagram below shows the structure of a nephron and its blood supply.

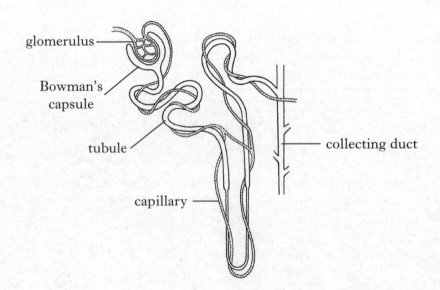

Describe how the nephron produces urine. There is no need to mention the role of ADH.

5

Question 2 is on *Page twenty-eight*.

SPACE FOR ANSWER TO QUESTION 1

DO NOT WRITE IN THIS MARGIN

Marks

2. Answer **either** A **or** B.

Labelled diagrams may be included where appropriate.

A. Plants living in the desert are adapted for survival. Describe **three** adaptations and explain how each adaptation increases the chances of survival of the plant. **5**

OR

B. Describe the structure of chromosomes. Explain how chromosomes determine the characteristics of an organism. **5**

[*END OF QUESTION PAPER*]

SPACE FOR ANSWER TO QUESTION 2

SPACE FOR ANSWERS

ADDITIONAL GRAPH PAPER FOR QUESTION 4(*a*)

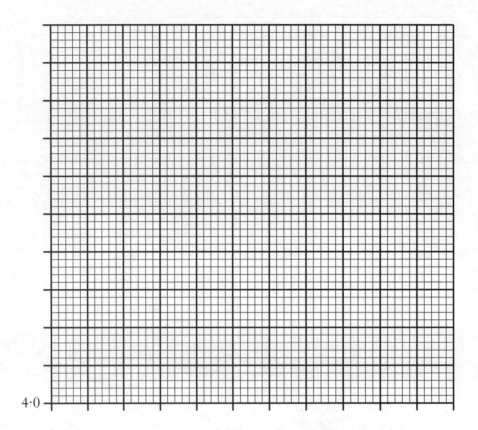

4·0

[BLANK PAGE]

FOR OFFICIAL USE

Total for
Sections B and C

X007/201

NATIONAL
QUALIFICATIONS
2005

WEDNESDAY, 18 MAY
9.00 AM – 11.00 AM

BIOLOGY
INTERMEDIATE 2

Fill in these boxes and read what is printed below.

Full name of centre

Cossiemouth High School

Town

Lossiemouth

Forename(s)

Jack G S

Surname

Smith

Date of birth
Day Month Year

Scottish candidate number

Number of seat

240797

SECTION A (25 marks)

Instructions for completion of Section A are given on page two.

SECTIONS B AND C (75 marks)

1   (a) All questions should be attempted.

     (b) It should be noted that in **Section C** questions 1 and 2 each contain a choice.

2   The questions may be answered in any order but all answers are to be written in the spaces provided in this answer book, and must be written clearly and legibly in ink.

3   Additional space for answers will be found at the end of the book. If further space is required, supplementary sheets may be obtained from the invigilator and should be inserted inside the **front** cover of this book.

4   The numbers of questions must be clearly inserted with any answers written in the additional space.

5   Rough work, if any should be necessary, should be written in this book and then scored through when the fair copy has been written. If further space is required, a supplementary sheet for rough work may be obtained from the invigilator.

6   Before leaving the examination room you must give this book to the invigilator. If you do not, you may lose all the marks for this paper.

Read carefully

1 Check that the answer sheet provided is for **Biology Intermediate 2 (Section A)**.

2 Check that the answer sheet you have been given has **your name**, **date of birth**, **SCN** (Scottish Candidate Number) and **Centre Name** printed on it.

Do not change any of these details.

3 If any of this information is wrong, tell the Invigilator immediately.

4 If this information is correct, **print** your name and seat number in the boxes provided.

5 Use **black** or **blue ink** for your answers. **Do not use red ink**.

6 The answer to each question is **either** A, B, C or D. Decide what your answer is, then put a horizontal line in the space provided (see sample question below).

7 There is **only one correct** answer to each question.

8 Any rough working should be done on the question paper or the rough working sheet, **not** on your answer sheet.

9 At the end of the exam, put the **answer sheet for Section A inside the front cover of this answer book**.

Sample Question

What must be present in leaf cells for photosynthesis to take place?

A Oxygen and water

B Carbon dioxide and water

C Carbon dioxide and oxygen

D Oxygen and hydrogen

The correct answer is **B**—Carbon dioxide and water. The answer **B** has been clearly marked with a horizontal line (see below).

Changing an answer

If you decide to change your answer, cancel your first answer by putting a cross through it (see below) and fill in the answer you want. The answer below has been changed to **B**.

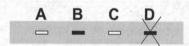

If you then decide to change back to an answer you have already scored out, put a tick (✓) to the **right** of the answer you want, as shown below:

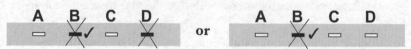

SECTION A

All questions in this Section should be attempted.

1. The diagram below represents a plant cell.

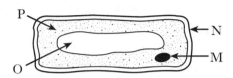

Which of the labelled parts of the cell are also found in an animal cell?

A   M and N

B   N and O

C   M and P

D   M, N, O and P

2. Which line in the table below describes correctly the functions of the cell wall and chloroplasts in plant cells?

	Function of cell wall	Function of chloroplast
A	prevents cell bursting	respiration
B	controls entry of substances	respiration
C	prevents cell bursting	photosynthesis
D	controls entry of substances	photosynthesis

3. When animal cells are placed in a hypotonic solution they

A   remain unchanged

B   burst

C   plasmolyse

D   become turgid.

4. A piece of potato was cut from a potato tuber and weighed. It was placed in pure water for an hour then removed, dried and weighed again. Finally, it was placed in a concentrated sugar solution for an hour, removed, dried and weighed again.

Which line in the table records the results most likely obtained by this treatment?

	First weighing	Second weighing	Third weighing
A	5 g	6 g	4 g
B	5 g	4 g	6 g
C	6 g	5 g	4 g
D	5 g	4 g	3 g

5. The anaerobic respiration of one molecule of glucose results in the net gain of

A   2 molecules of ATP

B   2 molecules of ADP

C   38 molecules of ATP

D   38 molecules of ADP.

[Turn over

6. The graphs below show the effects of temperature and pH on the activity of an enzyme.

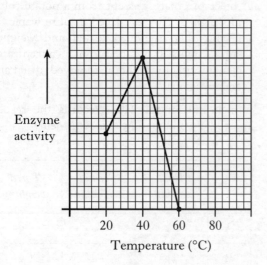

Temperature (°C)

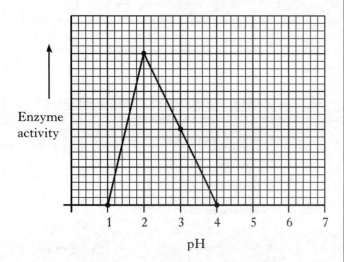

pH

Which line in the table identifies correctly the conditions at which the enzyme is most active?

	Temperature	*pH*
Ⓐ	40	2
B	40	4
C	50	2
D	60	4

7. The diagram below shows the respiratory pathway in an animal cell.

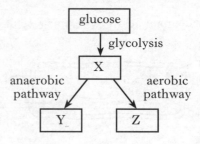

Which line in the table below identifies correctly X, Y and Z?

	X	*Y*	*Z*
A	lactic acid	pyruvic acid	carbon dioxide and water
B	carbon dioxide and water	pyruvic acid	lactic acid
C	pyruvic acid	carbon dioxide and water	lactic acid
Ⓓ	pyruvic acid	lactic acid	carbon dioxide and water

8. Photolysis is the

Ⓐ combining of water with carbon dioxide

B use of water by chlorophyll to split light

C release of energy from water using light energy

D splitting of water using light energy.

9. ATP synthesised during photolysis provides the carbon fixation stage of photosynthesis with

A glucose

Ⓑ carbon dioxide

C energy

D hydrogen.

10. Which of the following describes a community?

   A The total number of one species present

   B All the living organisms and the non-living parts

   C All the living organisms

   D All the plants

11. The bar chart shows the results of a survey into the heights of bell heather plants on an area of moorland.

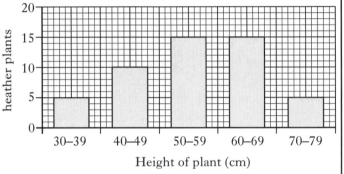

The percentage of plants with a height greater than 59 cm is

   A 15%

   B 20%

   C 30%

   D 40%.

12. A survey was carried out on numbers of mussels attached to rocks on a sea shore.

Squares measuring 10 cm × 10 cm were used in the survey.

The positions of the squares and the number of mussels in each square are shown below.

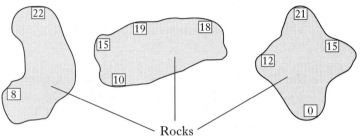

Rocks

How could the results have been made more valid?

   A Sample only one rock

   B Use bigger squares

   C Note all species present

   D Count each at the same time of day

13. Plants convert 1% of the light energy they receive into new plant material.

In the food chain below, plant plankton receive 100 000 units of light energy.

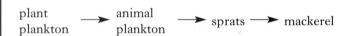

plant plankton → animal plankton → sprats → mackerel

How much of this energy is converted into new plant material?

   A 10 000 units

   B 1000 units

   C 100 units

   D 10 units

14. The DNA of a chromosome carries information which determines the structure and function of

   A fats

   B bases

   C carbohydrates

   D proteins.

[Turn over

15. A true breeding red bull is mated with a true breeding white cow. The offspring are all intermediate in colour (roan).

This type of inheritance is

A polygenic

B recessive

C co-dominant

D dominant.

16. In 1997, the USA planted 8·2 million hectares of land with genetically engineered crops. By 1998, this had increased to 20·5 million hectares.

What was the percentage increase in the area sown between 1997 and 1998?

A 12·3%

B 66%

C 150%

D 166·7%

17. In tomato plants, the allele for red fruit is dominant to the allele for yellow fruit.

If a heterozygous tomato plant is crossed with a plant which produces yellow fruit, the expected phenotype ratio of the offspring would be

A 3 red : 1 yellow

B 1 red : 3 yellow

C 1 red : 2 yellow

D 1 red : 1 yellow.

18. *Achoo syndrome* is a dominant characteristic in humans which causes the sufferer to sneeze in response to bright light.

A woman who is homozygous for the syndrome and a man who is unaffected have children.

What proportion of their children would be expected to have *Achoo syndrome*?

A 0%

B 25%

C 50%

D 100%

19. Genetic engineering can be used to alter bacterial cells in order to produce human insulin.

The stages in the process are:

1 insulin gene extracted from a human cell

2 bacteria divide and produce large quantities of human insulin

3 plasmid is removed from bacterial cell and "cut" open

4 insulin gene is inserted into bacterial plasmid.

The correct sequence of these stages is

A 1, 3, 4, 2

B 1, 3, 2, 4

C 3, 4, 2, 1

D 3, 1, 2, 4.

20. Food tests were carried out on different food samples. The results are shown below.

Food sample	Food Tests			
	Starch	*Glucose*	*Protein*	*Fat*
A	positive	negative	positive	positive
B	negative	positive	positive	positive
C	positive	negative	negative	positive
D	positive	positive	negative	negative

Which food sample left a translucent spot on filter paper and also turned brick red when heated with Benedicts solution?

21. Which food group contains the most energy per gram?

A Carbohydrate

B Protein

C Fat

D Vitamins

22. Stomach muscles relax and contract in order to

A release enzymes

B aid absorption of digested products

C release mucus and acid

D mix food with digestive juices.

23. The graph below shows the relationship between oxygen concentration and the concentration of oxyhaemoglobin.

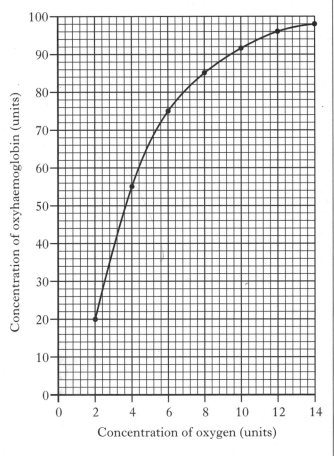

What is the percentage increase in the concentration of oxyhaemoglobin when the concentration of oxygen increases from 6 units to 12 units?

A 6

B 21

C 28

D 96

24. The diagram below shows a human brain.

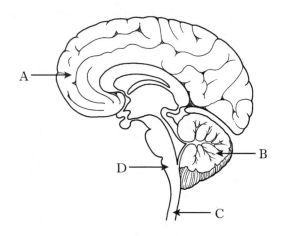

Which letter indicates the site of memory and conscious responses?

25. The diagram below shows the times taken in milliseconds (ms) for nerve impulses to travel along parts of the nervous system.

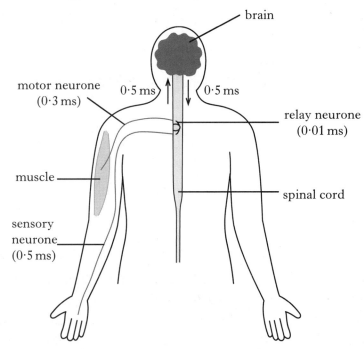

The time taken for a reflex response involving the nerves above is

A 0·81 ms

B 1·01 ms

C 1·80 ms

D 1·81 ms.

Candidates are reminded that the answer sheet for Section A MUST be placed INSIDE the front cover of this answer book.

[Turn over for Section B on *Page eight*

Marks

SECTION B

All questions in this section should be attempted.

1. The diagram below shows the human alimentary canal.

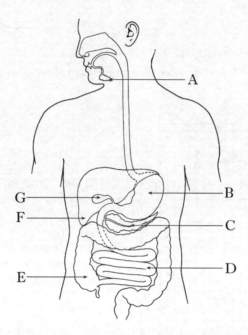

(a) Name the following labelled parts.

Letter	Name
A	
G	
E	

2

(b) Use a letter from the diagram to identify where each of the following secretions are **produced**.

Secretion	Letter
bile	
hydrochloric acid	
lipase	

3

(c) Excess glucose in the diet is converted into an insoluble compound which is stored in the liver. Name this compound.

_____

1

Marks

2. (*a*) The diagram below shows part of the human urinary system.

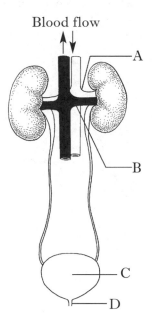

Blood flow

A

B

C

D

(i) Complete the table below to name the labelled parts and give their functions.

Letter	Name	Function
A	Renal artery	
C		
D		Carries urine out of the body.

3

(ii) Give **one** difference between the composition of blood in vessels A and B.

_____ **1**

(*b*) Glucose is present in the blood entering the kidney. Explain why glucose does not normally appear in the urine.

_____

_____ **1**

(*c*) (i) Name the hormone which is produced in response to a reduction in water concentration of the blood.

_____ **1**

(ii) State the effect this hormone has on the kidney tubules.

_____ **1**

Marks

3. The diagram below shows the apparatus used to investigate the energy content of different foods. One gram of each food was burned under a beaker containing $100\,\text{cm}^3$ of water.

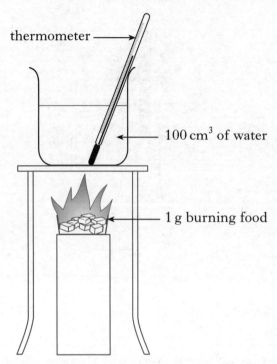

thermometer

$100\,\text{cm}^3$ of water

1 g burning food

The temperature rise for each food was recorded.
The energy content of the foods was calculated using the following equation.

energy content = temperature rise × 420 (joules/g)

The table below shows the results for the investigation.

Food	Energy Content (joules/g)
butter	10 500
chicken	4200
bread	3400
margarine	10 500

(a) Calculate the **simple whole number ratio** of the energy content of chicken to that of butter.
Space for calculation

_____ : _____   1
      chicken   butter

Marks

3. (continued)

(*b*) Construct a bar graph of the results given in the table.

(Additional graph paper, if required, will be found on page 26.)

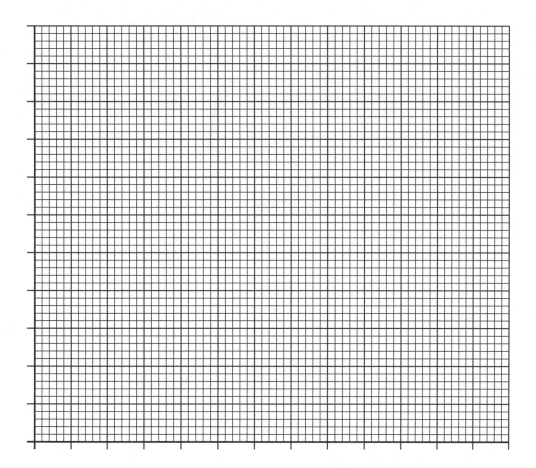

3

(*c*) One gram of fish was also burned. The temperature rise was 7·5 °C. Calculate the energy content for fish using the equation above.

Space for calculation

Energy content = _____ joules/g   **1**

(*d*) Slimmers may be advised to use margarine instead of butter. Use the data in the table to suggest why this would not aid weight loss.

_____   **1**

DO NC
WRITE
THIS
MARG

Marks

4. (*a*) The diagram below shows a surface view of the human heart.

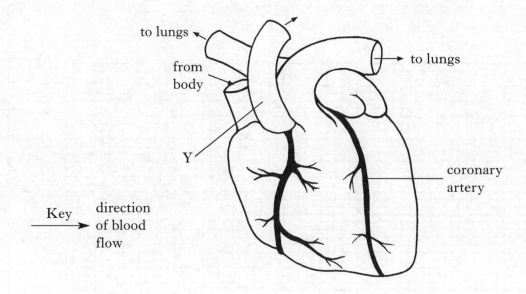

to lungs

from
body

to lungs

Y

coronary
artery

Key → direction
of blood
flow

(i) Name blood vessel Y.

_____   **1**

(ii) Name the blood vessel which carries blood to the lungs.

_____   **1**

(iii) If the coronary artery is blocked, the heart cannot function efficiently.

Name **two** essential substances carried by the blood which would be prevented from reaching the heart muscle.

1 _____

2 _____   **2**

Marks

4. (continued)

(b) The diagram below shows a type of blood cell which produces antibodies against disease-causing organisms.

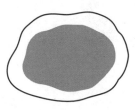

(i) Name this type of blood cell.

_____   1

(ii) Explain why each antibody is effective against only one type of disease-causing organism.

_____

_____   1

(iii) These blood cells produce antibodies when injections are given to protect against disease such as tetanus. Two injections may be given several weeks apart.

The following graphs show the antibody production in response to the two injections.

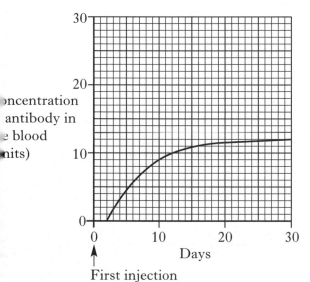

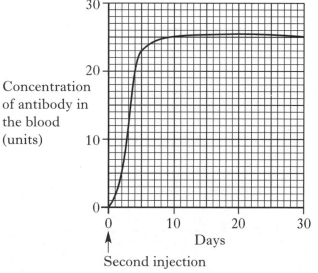

Give **two** differences in the antibody production in response to the two injections.

1 _____

2 _____   2

DO NO
WRITE
THIS
MARG

Marks

5. (*a*) The diagram below shows an air sac and a capillary in the lungs.

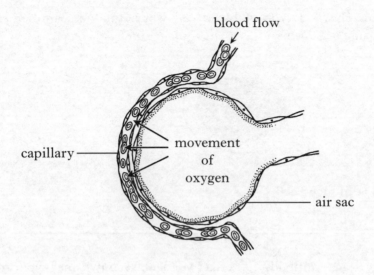

blood flow

capillary

movement
of
oxygen

air sac

(i) Name the process by which oxygen moves from the air sac into the capillary.

_____ 1

(ii) Why is oxygen required by an organism?

_____ 1

(iii) Complete the following sentence using the words "high" or "low".

Oxygen is moving from a _____ concentration in the air sac to a

_____ concentration in the capillary. 1

(iv) Name a substance which moves from the capillary into the air sac.

_____ 1

(*b*) Give **two** features of the air sacs which make them efficient gas exchange surfaces.

Feature 1 _____ 1

Feature 2 _____ 1

Marks

6. (*a*) Enzymes are involved in synthesis or degradation chemical reactions. The diagram below represents an example of one of these types of reactions.

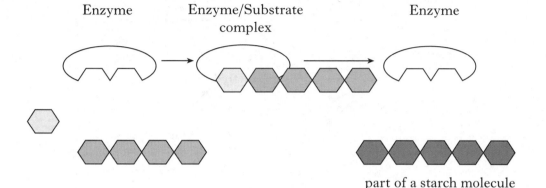

Enzyme   Enzyme/Substrate   Enzyme
                    complex

part of a starch molecule

    (i) Name the type of chemical reaction and the enzyme shown in the diagram.

        Type of chemical reaction _____

        The enzyme   _____   2

    (ii) Place an X on the diagram to show the position of an active site.   1

(*b*) What type of molecule are all enzymes made of?

_____   1

(*c*) What happens to the active site when an enzyme is denatured?

_____   1

(*d*) State the effect of an enzyme on the energy input needed for a chemical reaction.

_____   1

[Turn over

Marks

7. (*a*) The diagram below shows part of a food web in a freshwater ecosystem.

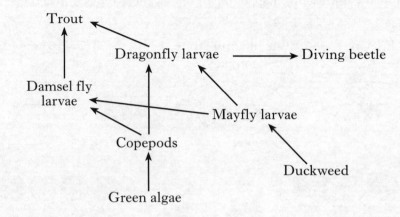

   (i) Use **four** organisms from the food web to construct a food chain below.

   _____ → _____ → _____ → _____   1

   (ii) Identify **all** the primary consumers in this food web.

   _____   1

   (iii) Draw and label a pyramid of numbers from the food web.

                                                        1

(*b*) What is meant by the term omnivore?

   _____   1

(*c*) What term is used to describe the variety of species within an ecosystem?

   _____   1

Marks

8. (*a*) The line graph below shows the decomposition of leaves in soil at different temperatures.

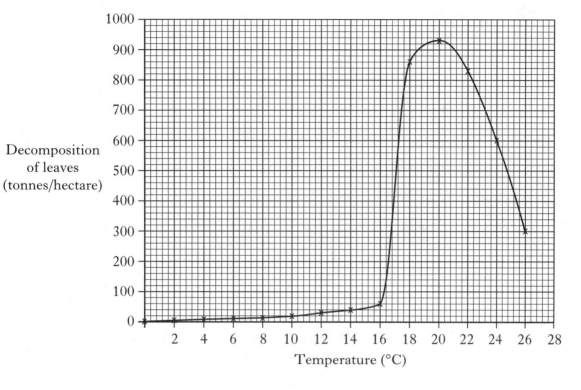

Decomposition of leaves (tonnes/hectare)

Temperature (°C)

(i) How many times greater is the decomposition of leaves at 24 °C than at 14 °C?

_____ 1

(ii) Describe the relationship between temperature and the decomposition of leaves.

_____

_____ 2

(*b*) Explain why temperature has an effect on the decomposition of leaves.

_____

_____ 1

(*c*) (i) Name **one** type of decomposer.

_____ 1

(ii) Describe the role of decomposers in the soil.

_____

_____ 1

Marks

9. (*a*) The table below shows the results of a study into the phenotypes of two pairs of human adult identical twins. Identical twins were used in this study as they have the same genotype.

One pair of identical twins had been raised together since birth.

The second pair had been separated since birth and raised by different families.

Phenotype	*Appearance of twins raised together*		*Appearance of twins raised apart*	
	P	Q	R	S
Eye colour	blue	blue	brown	brown
Height (cm)	175	174	180	176
Blood group	A	A	O	O
Hand span (cm)	23	23·5	25	23

From the results, complete the following table by using tick(s) to show whether each phenotype was affected by genes, the environment or both.

Phenotype	*Affected by genes*	*Affected by environment*
Eye colour		
Height		
Blood group		
Hand span		

2

(*b*) In another study into plant phenotypes, leaf lengths were found to vary across a wide range.

What term is used to describe this type of variation?

_____

1

Marks

9. **(continued)**

   (*c*)   The diagram below shows all the chromosomes found in a human skin cell.

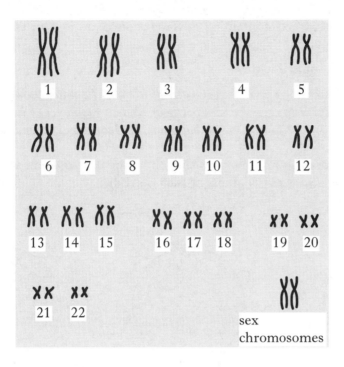

      Identify the sex of the person and give a reason for your answer.

      Sex _____

      Reason _____

      _____   **1**

   (*d*)   <u>Underline</u> **one** option in each set of brackets to make the following sentences correct.

      During meiosis, matching chromosomes pair and separate producing $\left\{ \begin{array}{l} \text{gametes} \\ \text{body cells} \end{array} \right\}$

      with $\left\{ \begin{array}{l} \text{one set} \\ \text{two sets} \end{array} \right\}$ of chromosomes. A zygote is produced from these cells

      by $\left\{ \begin{array}{l} \text{random assortment} \\ \text{fertilisation} \end{array} \right\}$.   **2**

[Turn over

Marks

10. The leaves of black walnut trees produce a chemical which is released into the soil when the leaves fall. This chemical prevents the germination (growth) of other plant seeds. The chemical can be extracted from the leaves.

(a) A student carried out an investigation into the effect of this chemical on mung bean seeds. Leaf extracts containing different concentrations of the chemical were prepared.

The student was supplied with

      30 mung bean seeds   *a bottle of 0·1% leaf extract chemical*
      3 identical petri dishes   *a bottle of 1% leaf extract chemical*
      cotton wool   *a bottle of 10% leaf extract chemical*

    (i) Complete the diagrams below to show how the investigation should have been set up. Label the contents of each petri dish.

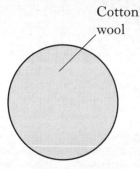 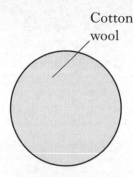 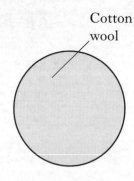

          Cotton   Cotton   Cotton
          wool   wool   wool

      Petri dish 1   Petri dish 2   Petri dish 3   **2**

    (ii) What observations and measurements should be taken to obtain results for this investigation?

_____

_____   **2**

    (iii) A control petri dish should also have been set up to show that it was the leaf extract preventing the growth of the mung bean seeds.

Complete the diagram below to show the contents of the control petri dish.

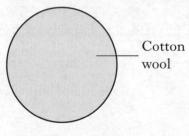

                            Cotton
                            wool

             Control petri dish   **1**

(b) Explain why producing this chemical is an advantage to the black walnut trees.

_____

_____   **1**

Marks

11. Charles Darwin visited the Galapagos Islands. He found different species of finch on the different islands.

The following gives information on the size and shape of beaks and the island habitats of two of the Galapagos finches.

Size and shape of beak	Habitat
Long and narrow	Rotting logs that provide food for insects
Short and wide	Trees and shrubs that provide seeds and nuts

Finch A   Finch B

(a) State which finch eats insects and give a reason for your answer.

Finch _____

Reason _____

_____   1

(b) Identify **two** ways in which competition between finch A and finch B is reduced.

_____

_____   2

[Turn over for SECTION C on *Page twenty-two*

Marks

SECTION C

Both questions in this section should be attempted.

Note that each question contains a choice.

Questions 1 and 2 should be attempted on the blank pages which follow.

Supplementary sheets, if required, may be obtained from the invigilator.

1. Answer **either** A **or** B.

   A. The diagram below shows some characteristics of two present day breeds of dog which descended from a wolf-like common ancestor.

   Name and describe the process which humans have used to produce different breeds of dog.

   5

OR

   B. The diagram below shows the two different forms of the peppered moth *Biston betularia* on the bark of a tree located in an unpolluted area.

   Name and describe the process by which the black form of the moth became the most common form in polluted areas of Scotland.

   5

Question 2 is on *Page twenty-four*.

SPACE FOR ANSWER TO QUESTION 1

[Turn over

DO NO
WRITE
THIS
MARGI

Marks

2. Answer **either** A **or** B.

Labelled diagrams may be included where appropriate.

A. Describe how cells are used in the production of yoghurt and alternative fuel. Include in your answer for both, the type of cell used, the substrates and the products.

5

OR

B. The rate of photosynthesis is limited by certain environmental factors.

Name **two** limiting factors and describe how the growth of greenhouse plants in winter can be increased.

5

[END OF QUESTION PAPER]

SPACE FOR ANSWER TO QUESTION 2

SPACE FOR ANSWERS

ADDITIONAL GRAPH PAPER FOR QUESTION 3(*b*)

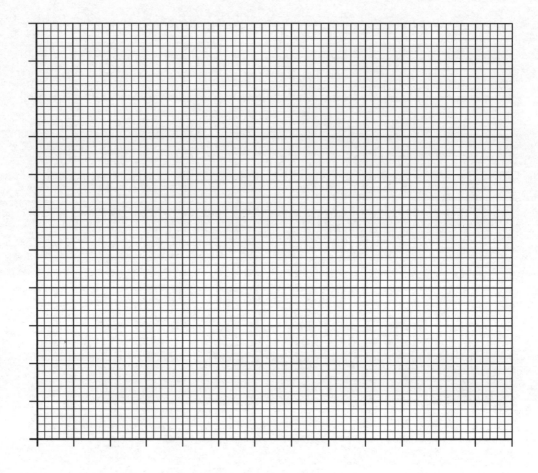

ADDITIONAL SPACE FOR ANSWERS

[BLANK PAGE]

[BLANK PAGE]

FOR OFFICIAL USE

Total for
Sections B and C

X007/201

NATIONAL QUALIFICATIONS 2006

TUESDAY, 23 MAY
9.00 AM – 11.00 AM

BIOLOGY

INTERMEDIATE 2

Fill in these boxes and read what is printed below.

Full name of centre

Town

Forename(s)

Surname

Date of birth
Day Month Year   Scottish candidate number   Number of seat

SECTION A (25 marks)

Instructions for completion of Section A are given on page two.

For this section of the examination you must use an HB pencil.

SECTIONS B AND C (75 marks)

1 (a) All questions should be attempted.

   (b) It should be noted that in **Section C** questions 1 and 2 each contain a choice.

2 The questions may be answered in any order but all answers are to be written in the spaces provided in this answer book, **and must be written clearly and legibly in ink**.

3 Additional space for answers will be found at the end of the book. If further space is required, supplementary sheets may be obtained from the invigilator and should be inserted inside the **front** cover of this book.

4 The numbers of questions must be clearly inserted with any answers written in the additional space.

5 Rough work, if any should be necessary, should be written in this book and then scored through when the fair copy has been written. If further space is required, a supplementary sheet for rough work may be obtained from the invigilator.

6 Before leaving the examination room you must give this book to the invigilator. If you do not, you may lose all the marks for this paper.

SCOTTISH
QUALIFICATIONS
AUTHORITY

©

Read carefully

1   Check that the answer sheet provided is for **Biology Intermediate 2 (Section A)**.

2   For this section of the examination you must use an **HB pencil** and, where necessary, an eraser.

3   Check that the answer sheet you have been given has **your name**, **date of birth**, **SCN** (Scottish Candidate Number) and **Centre Name** printed on it.

    Do not change any of these details.

4   If any of this information is wrong, tell the Invigilator immediately.

5   If this information is correct, **print** your name and seat number in the boxes provided.

6   The answer to each question is **either** A, B, C or D. Decide what your answer is, then, using your pencil, put a horizontal line in the space provided (see sample question below).

7   There is **only one correct** answer to each question.

8   Any rough working should be done on the question paper or the rough working sheet, **not** on your answer sheet.

9   At the end of the exam, put the **answer sheet for Section A inside the front cover of this answer book**.

Sample Question

Which substances are normally excreted in urine?

A   Urea and salts

B   Protein and urea

C   Glucose and salts

D   Protein and salts

The correct answer is **A**—Urea and salts. The answer **A** has been clearly marked in **pencil** with a horizontal line (see below).

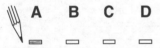

Changing an answer

If you decide to change your answer, carefully erase your first answer and using your pencil, fill in the answer you want. The answer below has been changed to **D**.

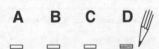

SECTION A

All questions in this Section should be attempted.

1. Which of the following prevents bursting of plant cells?

   A Nucleus

   B Cytoplasm

   C Cell wall

   D Cell membrane

2. Which of the following products is made using bacteria?

   A Yoghurt

   B Bread

   C Beer

   D Wine

3. Yeast respire anaerobically when there is a

   A high concentration of alcohol

   B low concentration of oxygen

   C high concentration of carbon dioxide

   D low concentration of sugar.

4. Respiration in yeast was investigated using the apparatus shown below.

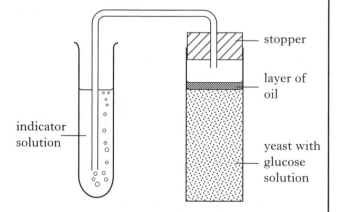

   Which of the following changes to the investigation would cause the yeast to respire more slowly?

   A Use cotton wool instead of a stopper

   B Do not add oil to the boiling tube

   C Change the indicator solution

   D Mix the yeast with water instead of glucose solution

5. The bar chart below shows the number of cells of different lengths in a sample of onion epidermis.

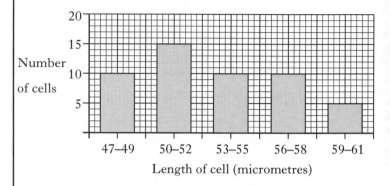

   The percentage of cells with a length greater than 55 micrometres is

   A 10%

   B 15%

   C 20%

   D 30%.

6. All enzymes are composed of

   A carbohydrates

   B protein

   C glycerol

   D fatty acids.

[Turn over

7. Two grams of fresh liver was added to hydrogen peroxide at different pH values.

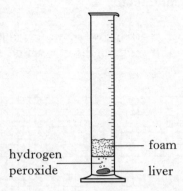

hydrogen peroxide — foam
liver

The time taken to collect 10 cm³ of oxygen foam was noted for each pH.

pH of hydrogen peroxide solution	Time to collect 10 cm³ of oxygen foam (s)
5	120
7	30
9	50
11	85

At pH 7, the enzyme which breaks down hydrogen peroxide is

A at its optimum activity

B at its minimum activity

C denatured

D digested.

8. The enzyme phosphorylase was added to a 2% glucose-1-phosphate solution. After one hour, the concentration of glucose-1-phosphate had fallen to 0·05%.

How many times lower was the concentration after one hour than at the start?

A   0·1

B   1·95

C   40

D   97·5

9. The table below shows the rate of photosynthesis by a plant measured at different light intensities.

Light intensity (kilolux)	Rate of photosynthesis (units)
10	2
20	27
30	51
40	73
50	82

What change in light intensity produces the greatest increase in the rate of photosynthesis?

An increase in light intensity from

A   10 to 20 kilolux

B   20 to 30 kilolux

C   30 to 40 kilolux

D   40 to 50 kilolux.

10. The word equation for photosynthesis is

A   carbon dioxide + water → glucose + oxygen

B   oxygen + water → glucose + carbon dioxide

C   glucose + oxygen → carbon dioxide + water

D   carbon dioxide + oxygen → glucose + water.

11. The diagram below shows an investigation into photosynthesis.

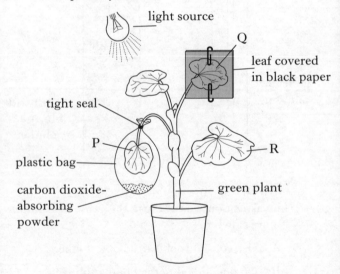

light source
Q
leaf covered in black paper
tight seal
P
R
plastic bag
carbon dioxide-absorbing powder
green plant

Which of the following statements is correct?

A   P, Q and R make food

B   only P and Q make food

C   only P makes food

D   only R makes food.

12. Plants compete mainly for

    A   water, light and soil nutrients

    B   water, food and soil nutrients

    C   light, water and food

    (D) light, food and soil nutrients.

13. The total variety of all living things on Earth is described as

    A   an ecosystem

    (B) biodiversity

    C   a community

    D   random assortment.

14. In Scotland, many forests are planted with a single species of tree such as Douglas fir.

    These forests have

    (A) a stable ecosystem

    B   complex food webs

    C   high intensity of grazing

    D   low insect species diversity.

15. Which of the following sets of conditions are likely to cause woodlice to move about most rapidly?

    A   Low humidity and low light intensity

    B   Low humidity and bright light

    C   High humidity and low light intensity

    (D) High humidity and bright light

16. A piece of potato weighs 20 g fresh and 5 g dry. What is the percentage water content of the potato?

    A   5%

    B   15%

    C   25%

    (D) 75%

17. The table shows water gained and lost by the body over a 24 hour period.

Method of water gain	Volume of water gained (cm^3)	Method of water loss	Volume of water lost (cm^3)
food	800	exhaled breath	300
drink	1000	sweating	
metabolic water	350	urine	1200
		faeces	100

What volume of water is lost by sweating?

    A   150 cm^3

    B   200 cm^3

    C   550 cm^3

    D   900 cm^3

18. Marine bony fish have to overcome an osmoregulation problem.

    Which line in the table describes how marine bony fish overcome this problem?

	Salts	Concentration of urine produced
(A)	absorbed	concentrated
B	excreted	dilute
C	excreted	concentrated
D	absorbed	dilute

19. Which of the following molecules is absorbed from waste food in the large intestine?

    A   Glucose

    B   Water

    C   Amino acids

    (D) Glycerol

[Turn over

20. Bile is produced in the liver and stored in the gall bladder.

Bile is released into the small intestine where it

A digests fat

B digests glycogen

C emulsifies fat

D emulsifies glycogen.

21. From what substance is urea manufactured and where does this process take place?

A From amino acids in the liver

B From amino acids in the kidney

C From fats in the kidney

D From fats in the liver

22. The bar chart shows the volume of blood supplied per minute to the skeletal muscles and to other parts of the body of a healthy male at rest and during strenuous exercise.

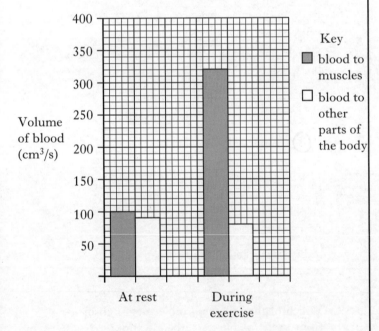

Key
- ▣ blood to muscles
- ☐ blood to other parts of the body

During **exercise**, the ratio of blood supplied to the muscles to blood supplied to other parts of the body is

A 1 : 4

B 4 : 1

C 10 : 8

D 10 : 9.

23. Which line of the table below identifies correctly the functions of macrophages and lymphocytes?

	Macrophages	Lymphocytes
A	produce antibodies	engulf bacteria
B	produce antibodies	produce antibodies
C	engulf bacteria	produce antibodies
D	engulf bacteria	engulf bacteria

24. The diagram below shows the neurones involved in a reflex arc.

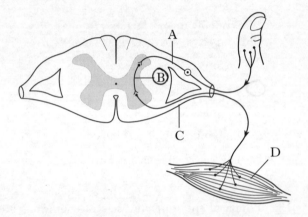

Which letter identifies the relay fibre?

25. Which of the following is a response to an increase in body temperature?

A Shivering

B Constriction of blood vessels

C Decrease in sweat production

D Dilation of blood vessels

Candidates are reminded that the answer sheet for Section A MUST be placed INSIDE the front cover of this answer book.

[Turn over for Section B on *Page eight*

Page seven

SECTION B

All questions in this section should be attempted.
All answers must be written clearly and legibly in ink

Marks

1. (*a*) Decide if each of the following statements about the breathing system is **True** or **False**, and tick (✓) the appropriate box.

If the statement is false, write the correct word in the **Correction** box to replace the word underlined in the statement.

Statement	True	False	Correction
The trachea divides into two <u>bronchioles</u>.	✓		
Air sacs are moist to allow <u>oxygen</u> to dissolve.		✓	Carbon dioxide
Large numbers of <u>capillaries</u> surround the air sacs.	✓		

3

(*b*) The following graphs show changes in lung pressure and volume during breathing in and breathing out.

Graph 1

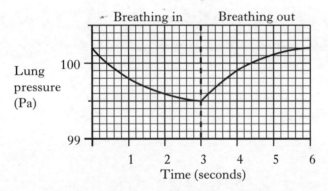

Graph 2

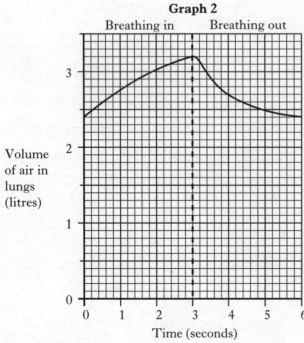

DO NOT WRITE IN THIS MARGIN

Marks

1. (*b*) continued

(i) From graph 2 calculate the volume of air breathed out in one breath.
Space for calculation

Volume = ________ litres **1**

(ii) State the relationship between lung pressure and the volume of the air in the lungs during breathing in.

As the volume of air increases, the lung pressure decreases. **1**

(iii) What evidence from graph 2 supports the statement that the lungs are never completely empty of air?

It shows that there is always over 2 litres of volume of air in the lungs. **1**

[Turn over

DO N
WRIT
TH
MAR(

Marks

2. (a) The diagram below shows the heart and its valves.

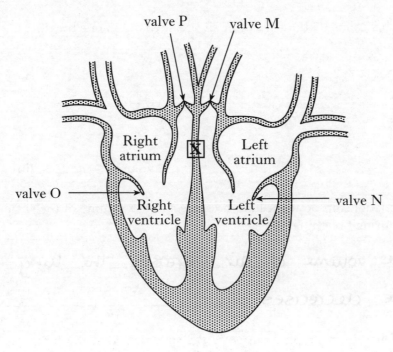

(i) What is the function of valves?

To regulate blood movement.

1

(ii) Give the letters of the **two** valves which would open as blood leaves the heart.

__N__ and __M__

1

(iii) At birth some babies have a hole at point X as shown on the diagram. What effect would this hole have on the oxygen concentration of the blood circulating around a baby's body? Explain your answer.

Effect   ~~That~~ It ~~oxy~~ would be less

1

Explanation It would not be oxygenated by the right ventricle.

1

Marks

2. **(continued)**

(*b*) The diagram below shows part of the human circulatory system.

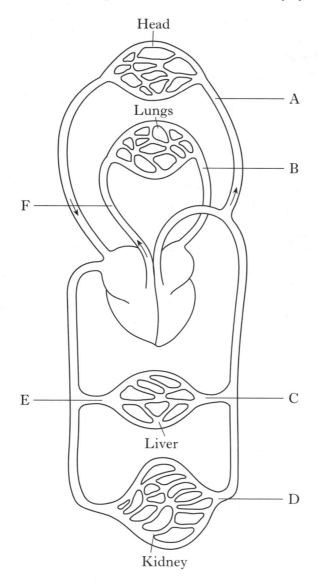

(i) Use information from the diagram to complete the following table.

Name of blood vessel	Part labelled
Renal artery	D
	B

1

(ii) Give **one** difference in the structure of arteries and veins.

Arteries are surrounded by capillaries.

1

[Turn over

DO NOT WRITE IN THIS MARGIN

Marks

3. (*a*) Amylase is produced in the salivary glands. The substrate of amylase is starch.

Amylase was added to a starch suspension and a sugar was produced.

(i) Name the sugar produced by the action of amylase on starch.

Glycogen **1**

(ii) State the optimum temperature for the action of amylase.

70 °C **1**

(*b*) An enzyme has a shape which is complementary to its substrate.

(i) What term describes this property of an enzyme?

Specific **1**

(ii) Name the part of the enzyme that is complementary to its substrate.

Active site **1**

Marks

.. graph below shows the energy content of equal masses of carbohydrate, fat and protein food types.

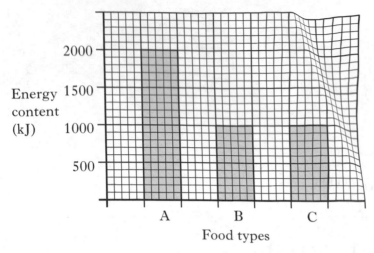

Food types

Identify food type A and give a reason for your answer.

Food type ___Carbohydrate___

Reason ___It has more energy content than fat + protein.___   1

(b) Biuret reagent is used to identify protein.

State the colour of a positive result for this food test.

___Black.___   1

(c) Name the element found in protein that is not present in carbohydrates and fats.

___Amino acids.___   1

(d) A healthy human diet contains a variety of minerals. Name one of these minerals and describe how it is used by the body.

Name ___Iron___

Description ___Helps in production of red blood cells___

___   1

[Turn over

5. (a) The diagram below shows a plant cell and an animal cell.

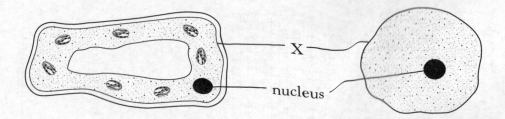

nucleus

    (i) Identify structure X.

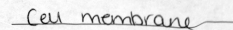

Cell membrane

                                                     1

    (ii) Give a function of the nucleus.

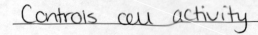

Controls cell activity

                                                     1

(b) Three plant cells P, Q and R are shown below.

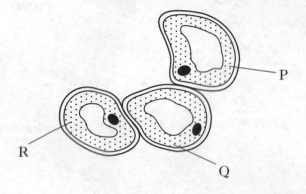

    (i) Cell P is hypotonic to cell Q and cell R is hypertonic to cell Q.

        Which cell has the highest water concentration?

        _R_

                                                     1

    (ii) If all three cells were placed in pure water for one hour, what term would be used to describe the resulting appearance of the cells?

        Plasmolysed

                                                     1

Marks

5. **(continued)**

(*c*) A biogas fuel generator is shown below.

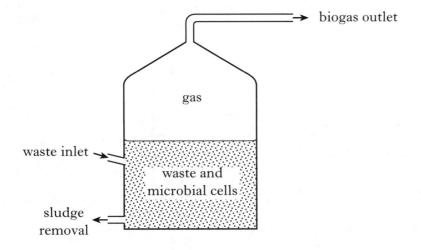

biogas outlet

gas

waste inlet →

waste and
microbial cells

sludge
removal ←

(i) What type of microbial cells produce biogas?

_____   1

(ii) Name the main gas collected at the biogas outlet.

<u>Carbon dioxide</u>   1

[Turn over

DO NO
WRITE
THI
MARG

Marks

6. The rates of photosynthesis and respiration in a green plant were measured over a period of 24 hours.

The results are shown in the graph below.

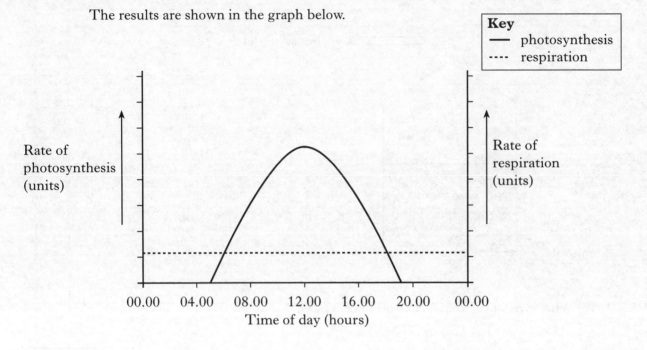

(*a*) (i) At what time was the production of glucose at its maximum?

12 · 00

1

(ii) Between what two times was the plant producing more oxygen than it was using?

Between 04·00 and 20·00 hours

1

(*b*) What substance traps the light energy required for photosynthesis?

Chlorophyll

1

Marks

6. **(continued)**

(c) The diagram below represents a summary of part of the process of photosynthesis.

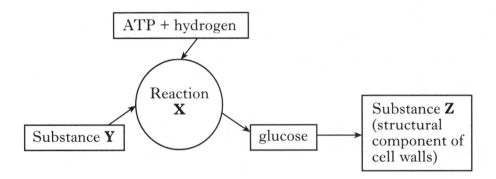

Name the following:

Reaction X Carbon fixation

Substance Y Carbon dioxide

Substance Z Cellulose

3

[Turn over

DO NO
WRITE
THIS
MARGI

Marks

7. (a) The diagram below shows part of an investigation into the effect of adding three different concentrations of ATP solution to three pieces of muscle.

Equal volumes of the ATP solutions were added to the pieces of muscle.

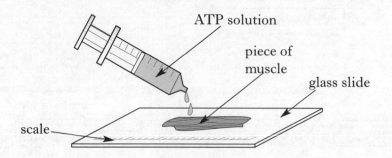

ATP solution

piece of muscle

glass slide

scale

The results are shown in the following table.

Concentration of ATP solution (g per litre)	Length of muscle			
	At start (mm)	After 10 minutes (mm)	Decrease (mm)	Percentage decrease
1	35	34·3	0.7	2
5	50	46	4	8
10	40	33	7	

(i) Calculate the percentage decrease in length of the muscle with 10 g per litre ATP solution.

Complete the table.

Space for calculation

$$33 \div 40 \times 100$$

1

(ii) In this experiment why is it necessary to use percentage decrease in length in the comparison of the results?

_____

_____ 1

DO NOT WRITE IN THIS MARGIN

Marks

7. (*a*) (continued)

(iii) Explain why three different syringes should be used in this investigation.

To rule out cross contamination as a ~~ta~~ limiting factor. **1**

(*b*) Muscle cells use energy for contraction.

State **one** other cell activity that uses energy.

~~Capillaries~~ Veins for contraction. **1**

[Turn over

Marks

8. (a) The diagram below shows a section of a river.

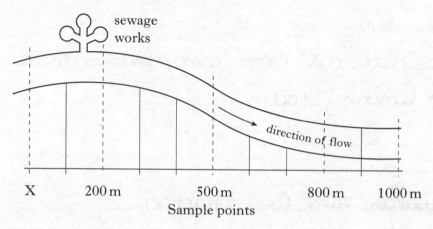

The table below shows the results of a survey into the oxygen content of the river at different sample points.

Distance of sample point from X (m)	Oxygen content (units)
0	1·20
200	0·04
500	0·20
800	0·40
1000	1·00

(i) Construct a **line graph** of the results given in the table.

(Additional graph paper, if required, will be found on page 34)

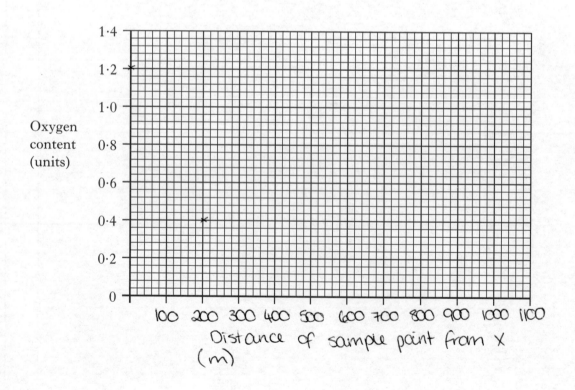

2

DO NOT WRITE IN THIS MARGIN

Marks

8. (*a*) (continued)

(ii) From the table calculate how many times greater the oxygen content is at 0 m than at 200 m.

Space for calculation

__________ times **1**

(iii) Use data from the table to describe the relationship between oxygen content and distance of the sample point from X.

____

____

____ **2**

(iv) The numbers of micro-organisms were counted at each sample point and found to be highest 200 m from X.

Account for the oxygen content of the river at 200 m.

____

____ **1**

(*b*) State the effect of an increase in pollution on species diversity.

____ **1**

[Turn over

Marks

9. (*a*) The diagram below shows part of a woodland food web.

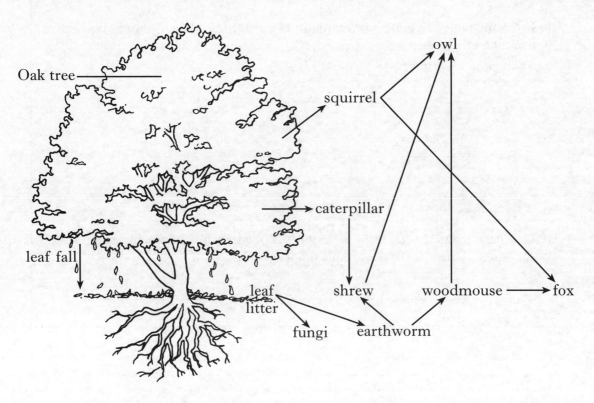

(i) Complete the table below using named examples from the woodland food web.

Type of organism	Named example
Producer	
Predator	
Decomposer	
Herbivore	

3

Marks

9. (*a*) **(continued)**

(ii)   The diagram below shows a **pyramid of numbers** taken from the food web above. Suggest a food chain, from the woodland web, which would give this pyramid.

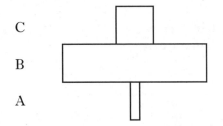

C

B

A

A_____ → B_____ → C_____   1

(iii)   Draw and label the pyramid of **biomass** for the following food chain.

leaf litter → earthworm → woodmouse → fox

1

(*b*)   State the term used to describe the role of an organism within an ecosystem.

_____   1

[Turn over

Marks

10. (a) Organisms vary from one generation to the next.
This variation may result from the following factors.

> A   Natural selection
> B   Selective breeding
> C   Environmental impact

Use this information to complete the table below.
(Each letter may be used once, more than once or not at all.)

Description	Factor
Produces changes not passed on to future generations	
Organisms that are better adapted to their surroundings survive and breed	
Effect of the surroundings on the final appearance of offspring	
Desirable characteristics chosen to produce improved offspring	

2

(b) Arrange the following stages of genetic engineering in the correct order.
The first stage has been given.

Stage number	Description of stage
1	Bacterial cell produces insulin
2	Insulin gene inserted into plasmid
3	Plasmid removed from bacterial cell
4	Plasmid inserted into bacterial cell
5	Insulin gene removed from human chromosome

Stage __5__ → _____ → _____ → _____ → _____

1

(c) Give **one** advantage of genetic engineering.

_____

_____

1

Marks

10. **(continued)**

(*d*) The desert plant shown below has adaptations to survive in dry conditions.

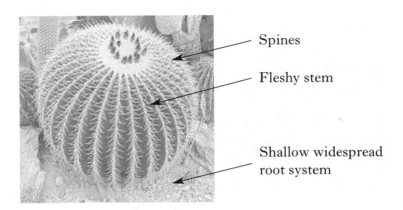

From the diagram give **one** adaptation which reduces water loss.

_____ 1

[Turn over

Marks

11. In humans the length of the big toe is controlled by a single gene which has two alleles.

A father is homozygous for short big toe. A mother has long big toes. All of their children have short big toes.

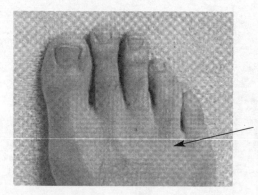

— Father's foot

(a) Complete the following sentences by **underlining** the correct word in each pair, using the information above.

$\left\{ \begin{array}{l} \text{Long} \\ \text{Short} \end{array} \right\}$ big toe is the dominant form of this gene. 1

The mother is $\left\{ \begin{array}{l} \text{homozygous} \\ \text{heterozygous} \end{array} \right\}$ and the children are all $\left\{ \begin{array}{l} \text{homozygous} \\ \text{heterozygous} \end{array} \right\}$. 1

Marks

11. **(continued)**

(b) The ability to roll the tongue is controlled by another gene in humans. The allele for tongue rolling (R) is dominant to the allele for non tongue rolling (r). The diagram below shows the occurrence of this tongue rolling gene.

Key

Female	Male	
◯	☐	tongue roller
◯ (shaded)	☐ (shaded)	non tongue roller

mother   father

Kate   Jill   Ben   Jamie

(i) With respect to the tongue rolling gene, state Jamie's phenotype and Ben's genotype.

Jamie's phenotype; _____   **1**

Ben's genotype.   _____   **1**

(ii) Kate has a son and his father is homozygous dominant for the characteristic.

What is the percentage chance that the son is a tongue roller?

Space for working

_____ %   **1**

(iii) State the two sex chromosomes present in Jill's body cells.

_____   **1**

[Turn over

Marks

12. (*a*)   The diagram below shows meiosis and fertilisation in humans.

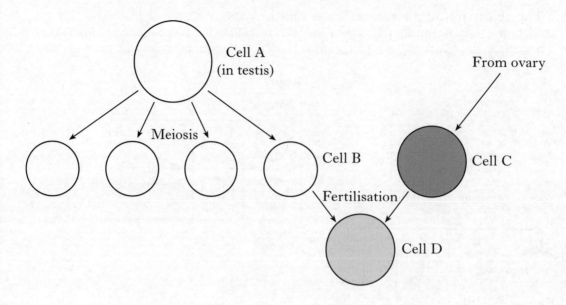

(i)   Complete the following table by naming the cells and stating the number of chromosomes present in each.

Cell	Name of cell	Number of chromosomes
A	testis cell	
B	sperm	
C		23
D		46

2

(ii)   Describe what happens during fertilisation.

_____

_____   1

(*b*)   (i)   Name a structure in a cell which is composed of a chain of DNA bases.

_____   1

(ii)   Explain the importance of the order of the DNA bases to the functioning of a cell.

_____

_____   1

[Turn over for SECTION C on *Page thirty*

Marks

SECTION C

Both questions in this section should be attempted.

Note that each question contains a choice.

**Questions 1 and 2 should be attempted on the blank pages which follow.
All answers must be written clearly and legibly in ink**

Supplementary sheets, if required, may be obtained from the invigilator.

1.   Answer **either** A **or** B.

  A.   The diagram below represents an animal cell that is respiring aerobically.

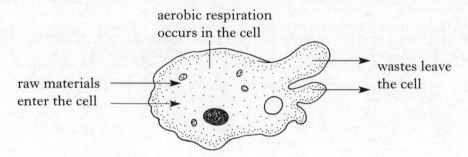

      Describe the **two** stages of aerobic respiration.   Include the names of the raw
      materials and the products of the two stages.   5

  OR

  B.   The diagram below represents an experiment set up as shown then left for
       1 hour.

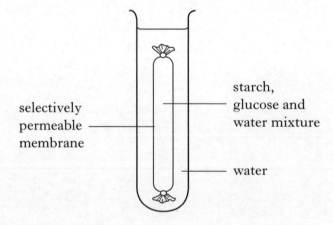

      Name and describe the **two** processes by which molecules would have moved.   5

Question 2 is on *Page thirty-two*.

SPACE FOR ANSWER TO QUESTION 1

[Turn over for Question 2
on *Page thirty-two*

DO NOT WRITE IN THIS MARGIN

Marks

2. Answer **either** A **or** B.

Labelled diagrams may be included where appropriate.

A. Describe the role of the small intestine in the digestion and absorption of food. **5**

OR

B. Describe the roles of the hypothalamus and ADH in the control of the water concentration of the blood. **5**

[*END OF QUESTION PAPER*]

SPACE FOR ANSWER TO QUESTION 2

DO NO
WRITE
THIS
MARG

ADDITIONAL SPACE FOR ANSWERS

ADDITIONAL GRAPH PAPER FOR QUESTION 8(*a*)(i)

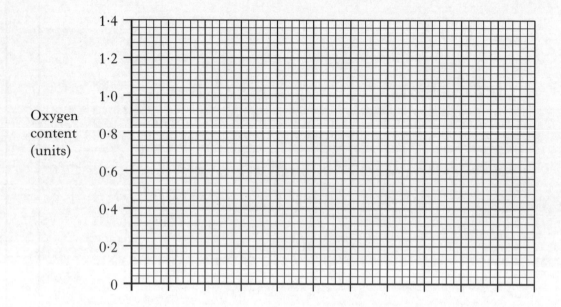

ADDITIONAL SPACE FOR ANSWERS

[BLANK PAGE]

[BLANK PAGE]

FOR OFFICIAL USE

Total for Sections B and C

X007/201

NATIONAL
QUALIFICATIONS
2007

MONDAY, 21 MAY
9.00 AM – 11.00 AM

BIOLOGY
INTERMEDIATE 2

Fill in these boxes and read what is printed below.

Full name of centre

Town

Forename(s)

Surname

Date of birth
Day Month Year   Scottish candidate number   Number of seat

SECTION A (25 marks)

Instructions for completion of Section A are given on page two.

For this section of the examination you must use an HB pencil.

SECTIONS B AND C (75 marks)

1   (a)   All questions should be attempted.

    (b)   It should be noted that in **Section C** questions 1 and 2 each contain a choice.

2   The questions may be answered in any order but all answers are to be written in the spaces provided in this answer book, **and must be written clearly and legibly in ink**.

3   Additional space for answers will be found at the end of the book. If further space is required, supplementary sheets may be obtained from the invigilator and should be inserted inside the **front** cover of this book.

4   The numbers of questions must be clearly inserted with any answers written in the additional space.

5   Rough work, if any should be necessary, should be written in this book and then scored through when the fair copy has been written. If further space is required, a supplementary sheet for rough work may be obtained from the invigilator.

6   Before leaving the examination room you must give this book to the invigilator. If you do not, you may lose all the marks for this paper.

SCOTTISH
QUALIFICATIONS
AUTHORITY

Read carefully

1 Check that the answer sheet provided is for **Biology Intermediate 2 (Section A)**.

2 For this section of the examination you must use an **HB pencil** and, where necessary, an eraser.

3 Check that the answer sheet you have been given has **your name**, **date of birth**, **SCN** (Scottish Candidate Number) and **Centre Name** printed on it.

   Do not change any of these details.

4 If any of this information is wrong, tell the Invigilator immediately.

5 If this information is correct, **print** your name and seat number in the boxes provided.

6 The answer to each question is **either** A, B, C or D. Decide what your answer is, then, using your pencil, put a horizontal line in the space provided (see sample question below).

7 There is **only one correct** answer to each question.

8 Any rough working should be done on the question paper or the rough working sheet, **not** on your answer sheet.

9 At the end of the exam, put the **answer sheet for Section A inside the front cover of this answer book**.

Sample Question

Plants compete mainly for

A   water, light and soil nutrients

B   water, food and soil nutrients

C   light, water and food

D   light, food and soil nutrients.

The correct answer is **A**—water, light and soil nutrients. The answer **A** has been clearly marked in **pencil** with a horizontal line (see below).

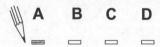

Changing an answer

If you decide to change your answer, carefully erase your first answer and using your pencil, fill in the answer you want. The answer below has been changed to **D**.

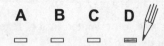

SECTION A

All questions in this Section should be attempted.

1. Which structural feature is common to both plant and animal cells?

   A   Cell wall

   B   Chloroplast

   C   Nucleus

   D   Large central vacuole

2. Which line in the table below correctly matches the plant cell structure to its function?

	Plant cell structure	Function
A	Cytoplasm	Controls all the chemical activities
B	Cell wall	Keeps the cells turgid
C	Vacuole	Prevents the cell from bursting in a hypotonic solution
D	Cell membrane	Controls which molecules enter or leave the cell

3. Once yoghurt has been produced it is stored in a fridge.

   This is because

   A   bacterial growth is slowed down

   B   it makes the yoghurt more creamy

   C   it causes lactose to change to lactic acid

   D   the taste of the yoghurt is improved.

4. The diagram below shows the results of an investigation into the effect of different antibiotics on a type of bacterium.

   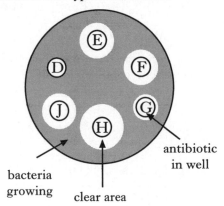

   Which of the following conclusions can be drawn from these results?

   A   These bacteria are resistant to antibiotic H.

   B   Antibiotic D is the most effective antibiotic against this type of bacterium.

   C   These bacteria are resistant to antibiotic D.

   D   This type of bacterium is resistant to all of the antibiotics.

5. The animals present in a sample of leaf litter were counted.

Animals	Number in sample
ground beetles	10
woodlice	35
slugs	5
centipedes	10
others	10

   What is the percentage of woodlice in the sample?

   A   35%

   B   50%

   C   65%

   D   70%

   [Turn over

6. The diagram below shows energy transfer within a cell.

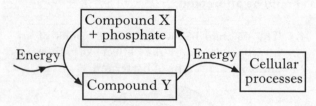

Which line of the table below identifies correctly compounds X and Y?

	X	Y
A	glucose	ATP
B	glucose	ADP
C	ADP	ATP
D	ATP	glucose

7. After running a race an athlete experienced muscle fatigue.

Which of the following had increased in the muscles?

A Glucose

B Oxygen

C ATP

D Lactic acid

8. Fermentation of sugar cane produces alcohol. What is produced when this alcohol is mixed with petrol?

A Biogas

B Gasohol

C Methane

D Carbon dioxide

9. Four cylinders of potato tissue were weighed and each was placed into a salt solution of different concentration.

The cylinders were reweighed after one hour. The results are shown in the following table.

Salt solution	Mass of potato cylinder (g)	
	Initial mass	Final mass
A	10·0	12·6
B	10·0	11·2
C	10·0	9·4
D	10·0	7·0

In which salt solution would most potato cells be plasmolysed?

10. An experiment was carried out to investigate the growth of pea plants kept in a high light intensity following germination.

The graph shows the average shoot length of the pea plants.

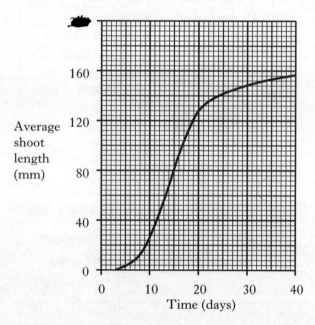

During which 5 day period is there the greatest increase in average shoot length?

A Day 10 – 15

B Day 15 – 20

C Day 20 – 25

D Day 25 – 30

11. The diagram below shows part of a food web in an oak woodland.

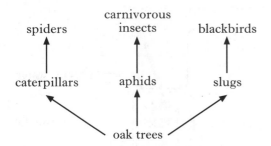

spiders   carnivorous insects   blackbirds

caterpillars   aphids   slugs

oak trees

The use of insecticides in a nearby field resulted in the deaths of most aphids and caterpillars.

Which line in the table identifies correctly the effects on the numbers of slugs and carnivorous insects?

	Number of slugs	Number of carnivorous insects
A	increases	decreases
B	decreases	stays the same
C	decreases	increases
D	increases	stays the same

12. The diagram below shows a pyramid of biomass.

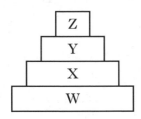

Z
Y
X
W

X represents the total mass of

A   producers

B   primary consumers

C   predators

D   secondary consumers.

13. Which of the following describes correctly a niche?

A   The place where an organism lives

B   Organisms and their environments

C   A population of organisms in an ecosystem

D   The role of an organism in an ecosystem

14. The table below shows the relationship between planting density and the mass of seed harvested for a cereal crop trial.

Planting density (number of plants per square metre)	Mass of seed harvested (grams per square metre)
4	60
8	86
15	105
32	77
128	21

What is the percentage increase in mass of seed harvested as planting density increases from 4 to 15 plants per square metre?

A   45%

B   75%

C   90%

D   105%

15. In humans, which of the following gametes are **not** normally formed?

A   An egg with an X chromosome

B   An egg with a Y chromosome

C   A sperm with an X chromosome

D   A sperm with a Y chromosome

16. The diagram below shows the same sections of matching chromosomes found in four fruit flies, A, B, C and D.

Fly A

Fly B

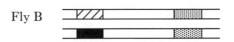

Fly C

Fly D

The genes shown on the chromosomes can be identified using the following key.

Key   gene for striped body
gene for unstriped body
gene for normal antennae
gene for abnormal antennae

Which fly is homozygous for both genes?

17. The diagram below shows a single villus from the small intestine.

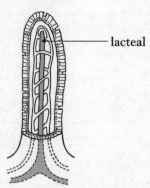

lacteal

Which food molecules are absorbed into the lacteal?

A   Amino acids and glycerol

B   Glucose and amino acids

C   Fatty acids and glycerol

D   Amino acids and fatty acids

18. Which line in the table below describes correctly the changes in food due to digestion?

	Changes in food	
	Molecule size	Solubility
A	decreases	increases
B	decreases	decreases
C	increases	decreases
D	increases	increases

19. The diagram shows the apparatus used to investigate the energy content of fat.

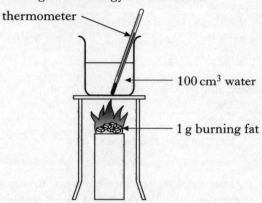

thermometer

100 cm³ water

1 g burning fat

Which of the experiments shown below allows a valid comparison to be made between the energy content of fat and protein?

A   B

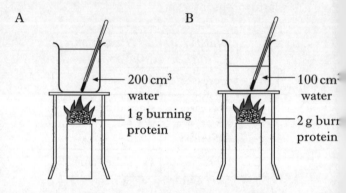

200 cm³ water
1 g burning protein

100 cm³ water
2 g burning protein

C   D

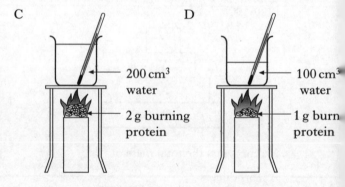

200 cm³ water
2 g burning protein

100 cm³ water
1 g burning protein

20. Bile is produced in the

A   liver

B   gall bladder

C   stomach

D   small intestine.

21. 100 g of baked beans contains 4·5 g of protein.

How many grams of beans would provide a daily protein requirement of 81 g?

A   5·5 g

B   18 g

C   364·5 g

D   1800 g

22. One way that marine bony fish cope with dehydration is

A   producing dilute urine

B   drinking seawater

C   producing large volumes of urine

D   absorbing salts.

23. The table below shows some features of blood vessels.

Which line describes features of veins?

	Direction of blood flow	Detection of pulse	Presence of valves
A	towards the heart	yes	no
B	away from the heart	no	yes
C	towards the heart	no	yes
D	away from the heart	yes	no

24. Which line in the table below identifies correctly how lymphocytes destroy bacteria?

	Phagocytosis	Antibody production
A	yes	yes
B	yes	no
C	no	yes
D	no	no

25. The graph below shows the relationship between the concentration of carbon dioxide and oxyhaemoglobin in the blood.

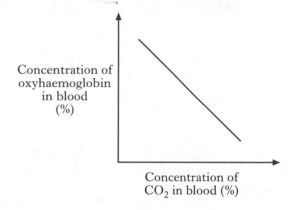

Which of the following describes this relationship?

A   As the carbon dioxide concentration decreases, the concentration of oxyhaemoglobin decreases.

B   As the carbon dioxide concentration increases, the concentration of oxyhaemoglobin decreases.

C   As the carbon dioxide concentration increases, the concentration of oxyhaemoglobin increases.

D   As the carbon dioxide concentration increases, it has no effect upon the concentration of oxyhaemoglobin.

Candidates are reminded that the answer sheet for Section A MUST be placed INSIDE the front cover of this answer book.

[**Turn over**

DO NO
WRITE
THIS
MARGI

SECTION B

Marks

All questions in this section should be attempted.
All answers must be written clearly and legibly in ink.

1. (a) The sentences below describe how oxygen enters the bloodstream for use in respiration.

   Underline one option in each set of brackets to make the sentences correct.

   Air entering the lungs passes down the $\begin{Bmatrix} \text{bronchioles} \\ \underline{\text{trachea}} \end{Bmatrix}$ to the bronchi.   1

   To collect oxygen, blood enters the lungs through the pulmonary $\begin{Bmatrix} \text{artery} \\ \underline{\text{vein}} \end{Bmatrix}$

   and returns to the $\begin{Bmatrix} \underline{\text{left}} \\ \text{right} \end{Bmatrix}$ atrium of the heart.   1

   (b) The diagram below shows an alveolus in the lungs.

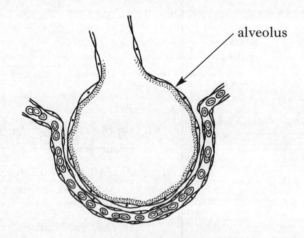

alveolus

   State **two** features of the alveolus that allow efficient gas exchange.

   Feature 1 _____   1

   Feature 2 _____   1

DO NOT WRITE IN THIS MARGIN

Marks

1. (continued)

(*c*) (i) Oxygen diffuses into muscle cells for respiration. Name **one** other raw material needed for respiration that enters by diffusion.

________________________ **1**

(ii) Name a waste product of respiration that diffuses out of muscle cells.

________________________ **1**

(*d*) Osmosis occurs in plant cells.

(i) Name the substance that enters or leaves cells by osmosis.

________________________ **1**

(ii) What term describes the condition of plant cells after being placed in distilled water?

________________________ **1**

[Turn over

Marks

2. (*a*) The experiment shown below was set up to demonstrate aerobic respiration in peas that are germinating (starting to grow).

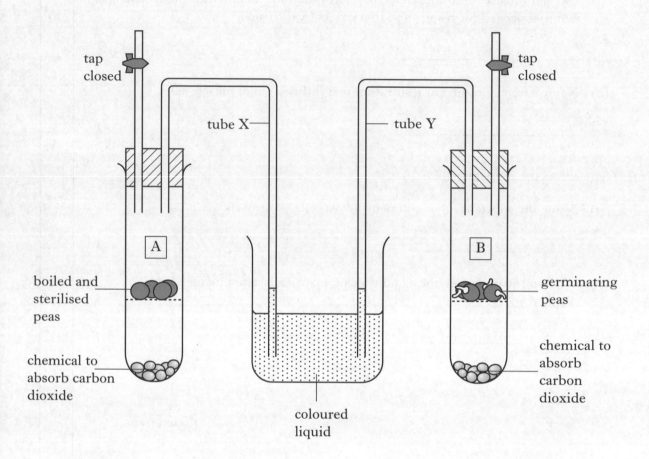

tap
closed

tube X

tube Y

tap
closed

A

boiled and
sterilised
peas

chemical to
absorb carbon
dioxide

coloured
liquid

B

germinating
peas

chemical to
absorb
carbon
dioxide

After two days, the level of liquid had risen in tube Y but had not risen in tube X.

  (i) Explain the purpose of A as a control in this experiment.

_____

_____   1

 (ii) Predict the effect on the level of the liquid in tube Y if a greater mass of peas is used.

_____   1

Marks

2. (continued)

(*b*) The following list contains some features of aerobic and anaerobic respiration in germinating peas.

List

W   Does not use oxygen
X   Produces carbon dioxide
Y   Yields 38 molecules of ATP per glucose molecule
Z   Produces ethanol

Complete the table below by writing the letters from the list in the correct columns.

Each letter may be used once or more than once.

Aerobic respiration in germinating peas	*Anaerobic respiration in germinating peas*

2

[Turn over

Marks

3. (*a*) A food sample was tested to find which food groups were present.
Both the Benedict's test and the Biuret test were positive.

   (i) What colour indicates a positive result with the Benedict's test?

   _____

                                                          1

   (ii) Which food group was indicated by the Biuret test result?

   _____

                                                           1

(*b*) Complete boxes 1 and 2 in the following diagram which shows information
about the structures of three food groups.

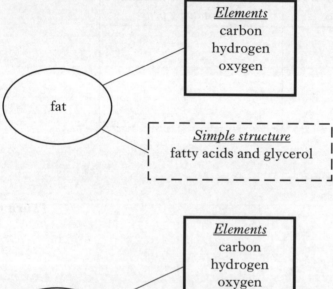

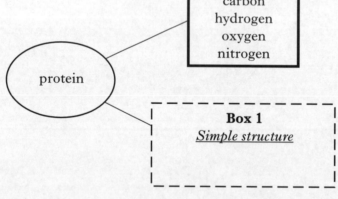

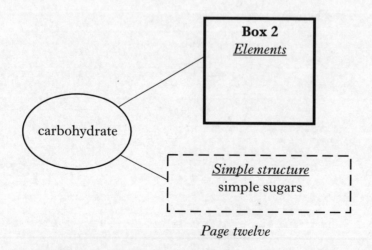

                                                          2

Marks

3. (continued)

(*c*) The graph below shows the results of an experiment into the activity of a stomach enzyme at various pH levels.

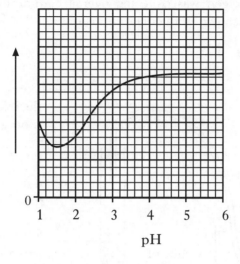

Mass of food
undigested after
24 hours
(grams)

pH

(i) Name a stomach enzyme.

_____   **1**

(ii) From the graph, what is the optimum pH of this enzyme?

pH _____   **1**

[Turn over

Marks

4. (*a*) Four groups of students investigated the catalase concentration of different tissues.

Each group set up a test-tube containing $5\,cm^3$ of hydrogen peroxide and a cube of potato. The oxygen was collected over a 3 minute period and the volume was measured as shown in the diagram below.

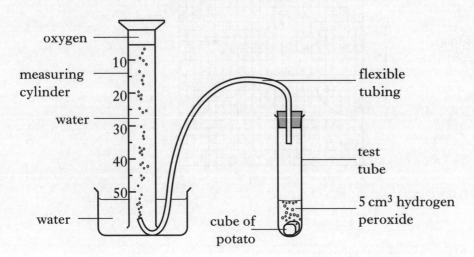

This procedure was repeated by each group using cubes of liver, apple and carrot. The results from the four groups are given in the table below.

Tissue	Volume of oxygen collected in 3 minutes (cm^3)				
	Group 1	Group 2	Group 3	Group 4	Average
Potato	5·5	5·0	5·5	6·0	
Liver	39·5	37·0	42·5	35·5	38·5
Apple	1·0	1·5	1·0	0·5	1·0
Carrot	3·5	3·0	3·5	2·0	3·0

(i) Complete the table to show the average volume of oxygen collected for potato tissue.

Space for calculation

1

(ii) The volume of hydrogen peroxide and time taken to collect the oxygen were kept constant in this investigation.

State **two** other variables that must be kept constant.

1 _____ 1

2 _____ 1

Marks

4. (*a*) **(continued)**

(iii) What was done in this investigation to make the results reliable?

_____

_____ 1

(iv) What conclusion can be drawn from these results?

_____

_____ 1

(*b*) The diagram below shows the action of the enzyme phosphorylase in a potato cell.

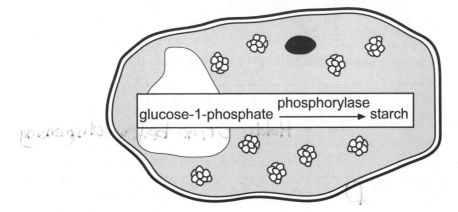

(i) <u>Underline</u> the option in the bracket to make the sentence correct.

The action of the enzyme phosphorylase catalyses the $\left\{ \begin{array}{c} \text{synthesis} \\ \text{degradation} \end{array} \right\}$ of

starch. 1

(ii) State the effect of phosphorylase on the rate of this reaction.

_____ 1

(iii) Explain why lipase could not produce starch in this reaction.

_____

_____ 1

[Turn over

Marks

5. (*a*) The diagram below shows the structure of the human urinary system.

Blood flow

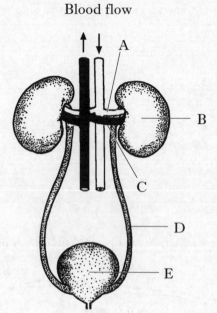

Complete the table to identify the structures and their functions.

Structure	Letter	Function
Bladder	E	Holds urine before dispensing
	A	Carries blood into the kidney
Ureter	D	Carries urine away from the kidney

2

(*b*) The diagram below represents filtration and reabsorption in the kidney.

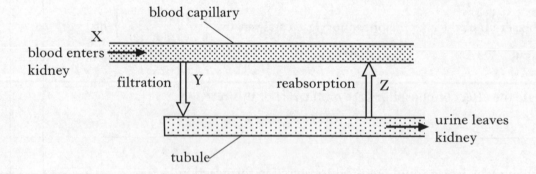

A hormone controls the volume of water reabsorbed at Z.

(i) Name this hormone.

_____

1

(ii) If there is a decrease in the level of this hormone, what will happen to the volume of water reabsorbed at Z?

_____

1

DO NOT WRITE IN THIS MARGIN

Marks

5. (*b*) (continued)

(iii) Tick (✓) the boxes in the table below to indicate which two blood components are filtered out of the blood at Y.

Blood components	*Filtered out at Y*
glucose	
salts	
blood cells	

1

(iv) The rate of flow at X, Y and Z is measured.

Rates of flow:

X = 1200 cm^3 per minute

Y = 125 cm^3 per minute

Z = 124 cm^3 per minute

How much urine will be produced in one hour?

Space for calculation

Volume of urine produced in one hour ____________ cm^3 **1**

[Turn over

Marks

6. The three types of neurone involved in the reflex arc for blinking are shown in the diagram below.

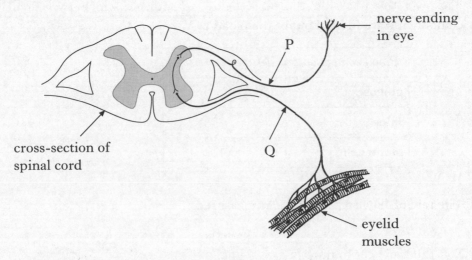

nerve ending
in eye

P

cross-section of
spinal cord

Q

eyelid
muscles

(*a*) Name neurones P and Q.

P _____

Q _____   2

(*b*) Which labelled structure is the effector in this response?

_____   1

(*c*) What is the function of a reflex action?

_____

_____   1

[Turn over for Question 7 on *Page twenty*

Marks

7. (a) An experiment was set up to measure the effect of light intensity on the rate of photosynthesis in the water plant, *Elodea*.
The light intensity was varied using a dimmer switch on the bulb.
The rate of photosynthesis was measured by counting the number of bubbles released per minute.

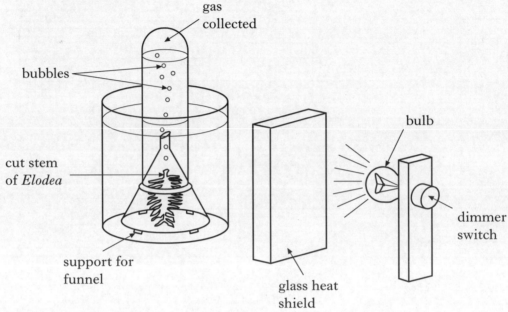

(i) Name the gas collected.

_____

1

(ii) The results of the experiment are shown in the table below.

Light intensity (units)	Rate of photosynthesis (number of bubbles per minute)
1	2
3	10
5	23
8	45
10	45
12	45

Marks

7. (*a*) (ii) (continued)

(A) On the grid below, plot a line graph to show rate of photosynthesis against light intensity.

(Additional graph paper, if required, will be found on page 32.)

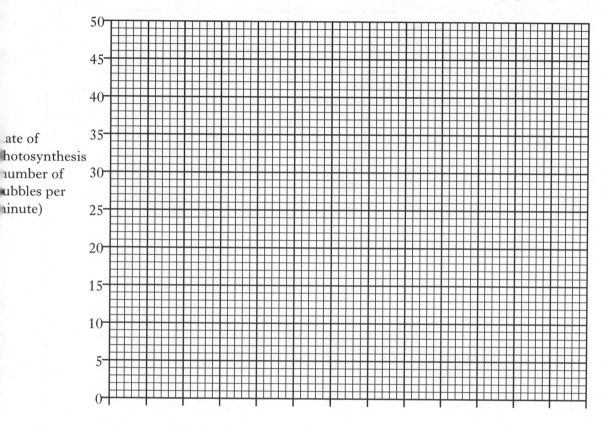

ate of
hotosynthesis
umber of
ubbles per
inute)

2

(B) Using the data in the table, explain the results obtained at light intensities greater than 8 units.

_____

_____ 1

(*b*) There are **two** reactions in photosynthesis. The first reaction is photolysis.

(i) Name the two substances produced by photolysis that are required for the second reaction.

Substance 1 _____

Substance 2 _____ 2

(ii) Name the second reaction.

_____ 1

DO NOT WRITE IN THIS MARGIN

Marks

7. (continued)

(*c*) Plant cells convert glucose into other carbohydrates.

Complete the table below by naming two of these carbohydrates.

Role of carbohydrate in plant cells	*Name of carbohydrate*
Storage as an insoluble material	
Forms cell walls	

2

Marks

8. (*a*) The diagram below shows a yeast cell.

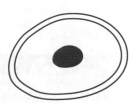

   (i) Name the structure shown in the yeast cell which contains the genetic information.

_____

1

   (ii) A molecule consisting of chains of bases is contained in chromosomes.

   (A) Name this molecule.

_____

1

   (B) Explain how this molecule controls cell activities.

_____

_____

_____

2

(*b*) Gamete production is essential to sexual reproduction.

   (i) Name the division of the nucleus that occurs during gamete production.

_____

1

   (ii) Name the process occurring during this division that increases variation.

_____

1

   (iii) <u>Underline</u> **one** option in each set of brackets to make the following sentences correct.

The number of chromosomes in gametes is $\begin{Bmatrix} \text{half} \\ \text{twice} \end{Bmatrix}$ the number found in

body cells.

The zygote is formed by $\begin{Bmatrix} \text{fusion} \\ \text{division} \end{Bmatrix}$ and contains $\begin{Bmatrix} \text{half} \\ \text{twice} \end{Bmatrix}$ the number of

chromosomes in a gamete.

2

Marks

9. In fowl, the dominant form (R) of one gene determines rose comb shape; single comb shape results from the recessive form (r) of the gene.

The diagram below shows the results of two crosses.

Cross 1 parents	True-breeding rose comb fowl		True-breeding single comb fowl
Cross 1 offspring		all rose comb fowl	
Cross 2 parents	Rose comb fowl from Cross 1 offspring	×	Single comb fowl
Cross 2 offspring	Rose comb fowl		Single comb fowl
Ratio	1	:	1

(a) (i) Which offspring contains only one phenotype?

_____

1

(ii) Complete the Punnet square below to show the genotypes of the gametes of the Cross 2 single comb parent and the genotypes of the offspring produced.

		Genotypes of gametes of Cross 2 single comb parent	
Genotypes of gametes of Cross 2 rose comb parent	R		
	r		

2

Page twenty-four

Marks

9. **(continued)**

   (*b*) Decide if each of the following statements is **True** or **False**, and tick (✓) the appropriate box.

   If the statement is **False**, write the correct word in the **Correction** box to replace the word underlined in the statement.

Statement	True	False	Correction
A characteristic controlled by many genes is called <u>co-dominant</u>.			
The <u>gene</u> for comb shape has two different alleles.			
True breeding is another way of describing a <u>homozygous</u> individual.			

3

[Turn over

DO NO
WRITE
THI
MARG

Marks

10. The small burrowing invertebrate, *Corophium*, is found in the mud of Scottish estuaries.

Corophium (magnified × 6)

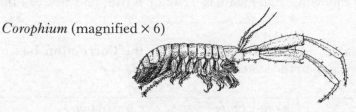

Corophium is the major prey of many species of migratory wading birds. These birds are present in large numbers from August to April.

The graph below shows the results of a one year survey on the numbers of *Corophium* taken on the first day of each month.

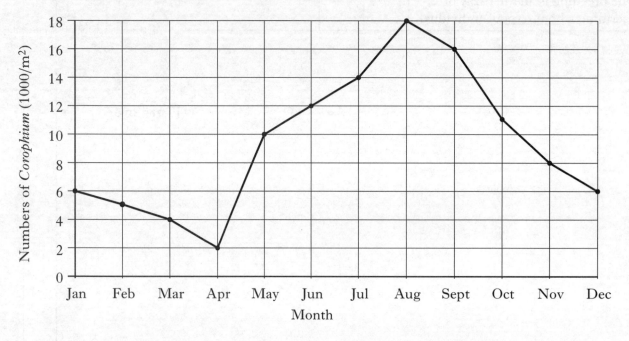

(a) Describe the changes in the numbers of *Corophium* from January to December.

_____

_____

_____   2

(b) How many times greater are the numbers of *Corophium* on 1st June compared to 1st April?

Space for calculation

_____ times   1

DO NOT WRITE IN THIS MARGIN

Marks

10. (continued)

(*c*) Using all the information given, explain why there are high numbers of *Corophium* on 1st August.

____

____ **1**

(*d*) Predict what would happen to the biodiversity of this estuary if the wading birds stayed all year. Explain your answer.

Prediction ____ **1**

Explanation ____

____ **1**

[Turn over for Section C on *page twenty-eight*

Marks

SECTION C

Both questions in this section should be attempted.

Note that each question contains a choice.

**Questions 1 and 2 should be attempted on the blank pages which follow.
All answers must be written clearly and legibly in ink.**

Supplementary sheets, if required, may be obtained from the invigilator.

1. Answer **either** A **or** B.

A. The diagram below shows human blood as seen through a microscope.

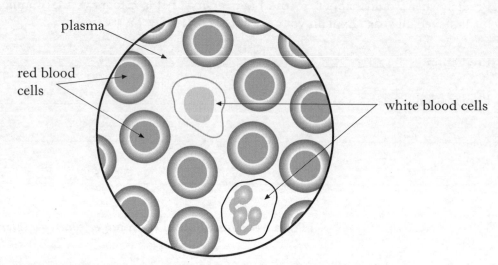

(a) Name the **two** parts of the blood involved in the transport of substances around the body.

(b) Describe how named substances are transported by each part of the blood.   **5**

OR

B. The diagram below shows a section through the brain.

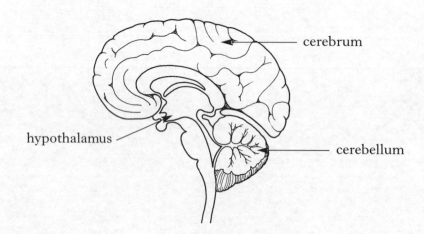

(a) Name the part of the brain that regulates body temperature.

(b) State its response to a **decrease** in body temperature by describing the changes which will occur in the skin, blood vessels and muscles.   **5**

Question 2 is on *Page thirty*.

SPACE FOR ANSWER TO QUESTION 1

[Turn over for Question 2 on *Page thirty*

Marks

2. Answer **either** A **or** B.

   Labelled diagrams may be included where appropriate.

   A. Genetic engineering uses bacteria to produce human insulin. Describe the stages involved in this process.   **5**

   OR

   B. Describe the process of natural selection as illustrated by the peppered moth *Biston betularia*.   **5**

[END OF QUESTION PAPER]

DO NOT
WRITE IN
THIS
MARGIN

SPACE FOR ANSWER TO QUESTION 2

ADDITIONAL SPACE FOR ANSWERS

ADDITIONAL GRAPH PAPER FOR QUESTION 7(*a*)(ii)A

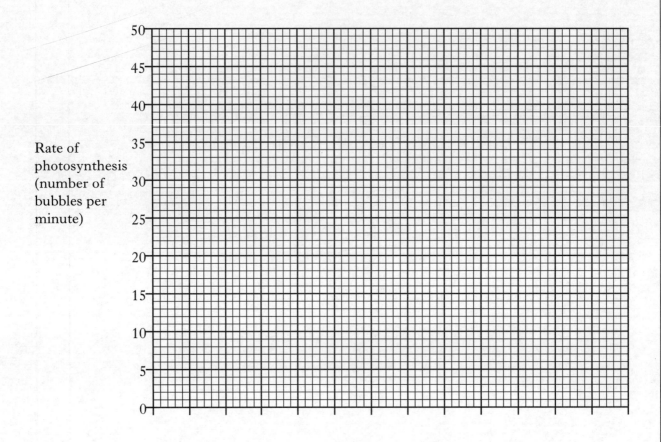

Rate of photosynthesis (number of bubbles per minute)

DO NOT
WRITE IN
THIS
MARGIN

ADDITIONAL SPACE FOR ANSWERS

DO NO
WRITE
THIS
MARGI

ADDITIONAL SPACE FOR ANSWERS

[BLANK PAGE]

FOR OFFICIAL USE

Total for
Sections B and C

X007/201

NATIONAL
QUALIFICATIONS
2008

TUESDAY, 27 MAY
9.00 AM – 11.00 AM

BIOLOGY

INTERMEDIATE 2

Fill in these boxes and read what is printed below.

Full name of centre

Town

Forename(s)

Surname

Date of birth

Day Month Year   Scottish candidate number   Number of seat

SECTION A (25 marks)

Instructions for completion of Section A are given on page two.

For this section of the examination you must use an HB pencil.

SECTIONS B AND C (75 marks)

1   (a) All questions should be attempted.

    (b) It should be noted that in **Section C** questions 1 and 2 each contain a choice.

2   The questions may be answered in any order but all answers are to be written in the spaces provided in this answer book, **and must be written clearly and legibly in ink**.

3   Additional space for answers will be found at the end of the book. If further space is required, supplementary sheets may be obtained from the invigilator and should be inserted inside the **front** cover of this book.

4   The numbers of questions must be clearly inserted with any answers written in the additional space.

5   Rough work, if any should be necessary, should be written in this book and then scored through when the fair copy has been written. If further space is required, a supplementary sheet for rough work may be obtained from the invigilator.

6   Before leaving the examination room you must give this book to the invigilator. If you do not, you may lose all the marks for this paper.

Read carefully

1 Check that the answer sheet provided is for **Biology Intermediate 2 (Section A)**.

2 For this section of the examination you must use an **HB pencil** and, where necessary, an eraser.

3 Check that the answer sheet you have been given has **your name**, **date of birth**, **SCN** (Scottish Candidate Number) and **Centre Name** printed on it.

   Do not change any of these details.

4 If any of this information is wrong, tell the Invigilator immediately.

5 If this information is correct, **print** your name and seat number in the boxes provided.

6 The answer to each question is **either** A, B, C or D. Decide what your answer is, then, using your pencil, put a horizontal line in the space provided (see sample question below).

7 There is **only one correct** answer to each question.

8 Any rough working should be done on the question paper or the rough working sheet, **not** on your answer sheet.

9 At the end of the exam, put the **answer sheet for Section A inside the front cover of this answer book**.

Sample Question

Plants compete mainly for

A   water, light and soil nutrients

B   water, food and soil nutrients

C   light, water and food

D   light, food and soil nutrients.

The correct answer is **A**—water, light and soil nutrients. The answer **A** has been clearly marked in **pencil** with a horizontal line (see below).

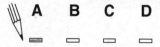

Changing an answer

If you decide to change your answer, carefully erase your first answer and using your pencil, fill in the answer you want. The answer below has been changed to **D**.

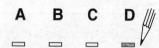

SECTION A

All questions in this Section should be attempted.

1. The diagrams below show four cells.

   Which cell is a leaf mesophyll cell?

   A
   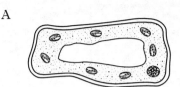

   B
   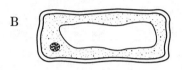

   C
   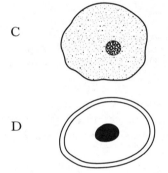

   D

2. Which line in the table below identifies correctly the importance of diffusion to an animal cell?

	Raw material gained	Waste product removed
A	oxygen	glucose
B	carbon dioxide	oxygen
C	oxygen	carbon dioxide
D	glucose	oxygen

3. Which of the following molecules can both diffuse through a cell membrane?

   A Amino acids and starch

   B Amino acids and water

   C Starch and protein

   D Protein and water

4. Red blood cells burst when they are placed in water because

   A the cell contents are hypotonic to the water

   B the cell contents are isotonic to the water

   C the water is hypotonic to the cell contents

   D the water is hypertonic to the cell contents.

5. The energy yield per glucose molecule during aerobic respiration is

   A 2 molecules of ATP

   B 18 molecules of ATP

   C 36 molecules of ATP

   D 38 molecules of ATP.

6. The following are statements about respiration.

   1 ATP is produced

   2 Lactic acid is produced

   3 Carbon dioxide is produced

   4 Ethanol is produced

   Which of the statements are true of anaerobic respiration in human muscle tissue?

   A 2 only

   B 2 and 3 only

   C 1 and 2 only

   D 1, 3 and 4 only

7. The role of chlorophyll in photosynthesis is to trap

   A light energy for ATP production

   B chemical energy for ATP production

   C light energy for ADP production

   D chemical energy for ADP production.

8. The raw materials for photosynthesis are

   A carbon dioxide and water

   B oxygen and water

   C carbon dioxide and glucose

   D oxygen and glucose.

9. All proteins are composed of

A genes

B DNA

C amino acids

D bases.

10. Which of the following diagrams best represents the arrangement of chromosomes in a cell undergoing meiosis?

A

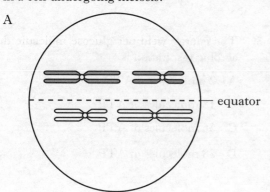

B

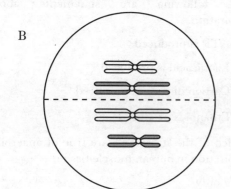

C

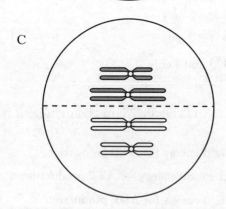

D

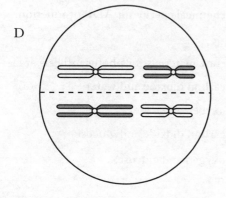

11. Which line in the table describes correctly the possible chromosome content of human gametes?

	Sperm		Ovum (egg)	
	Total number of chromosomes	Type of sex chromosome	Total number of chromosomes	Type of sex chromosome
A	23	X	23	Y
B	23	Y	23	X
C	46	X	46	Y
D	46	Y	46	X

12. In the fruit fly *Drosophila*, the allele for normal wings is dominant to the allele for short wings.

A normal winged fly was crossed with a short winged fly and all the F_1 offspring had normal wings.

If these F_1 offspring were to mate with each other, what percentage of the F_2 offspring would be expected to have normal wings?

A 25%

B 50%

C 75%

D 100%

13. The diagram below shows the same sections of matching chromosomes found in four fruit flies, A, B, C and D.

The genes shown on the chromosomes can be identified using the following key.

Key   ▨ dominant gene for striped body

      ■ recessive gene for unstriped body

      ▦ dominant gene for normal antennae

      ▩ recessive gene for abnormal antennae

Which fly has a striped body and abnormal antennae?

14. In a breed of dog, the alleles for white coat colour and black coat colour are **co-dominant**.

A cross was performed between two heterozygous dogs.

Which line in the table below shows the numbers of different phenotypes and genotypes which are possible in the offspring?

	Number of phenotypes	Number of genotypes
A	1	3
B	2	3
C	3	2
D	3	3

15. Which of the following is an example of natural selection?

A   Increased milk yield in dairy cattle

B   Industrial melanism in Peppered Moths

C   Insulin production by bacteria

D   Insertion of DNA into a chromosome

16. The Peppered Moth is found in two distinct forms. One form is dark coloured and the other is light coloured. The moths rest on the trunks of trees.

Pale coloured tree-trunks in an area were darkened by pollution. What would happen to the numbers of the two forms of the Peppered Moth in that area?

A   The numbers of each form would increase.

B   The dark form would increase and the light form decrease.

C   The numbers of each form would decrease.

D   The light form would increase and the dark form decrease.

17. Which of the following is **not** a benefit of selective breeding in crop plants?

A   Higher yields can be produced.

B   Undesirable features can be eliminated.

C   Seed quality can be improved.

D   Higher yields can always be guaranteed.

18. Lipase is an enzyme found in the small intestine. Lipase speeds up the breakdown of fat. Full cream milk contains a high proportion of fat.

Three test tubes were set up as shown in the diagram below.

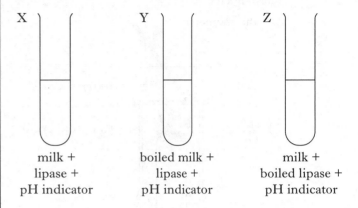

milk + lipase + pH indicator

boiled milk + lipase + pH indicator

milk + boiled lipase + pH indicator

The pH of the contents of each test tube was recorded at the start and again 15 minutes later.

What changes in pH took place?

A   The pH decreased in each test tube.

B   The pH increased in each test tube.

C   The pH decreased in tubes X and Y and did not change in tube Z.

D   The pH increased in tubes Y and Z and did not change in tube X.

[Turn over

19. The diagram below shows the apparatus used to investigate the energy contents of different foods.

1 g of each food was burned under a beaker containing $100 \, cm^3$ of water. The rise in water temperature was measured using a thermometer.

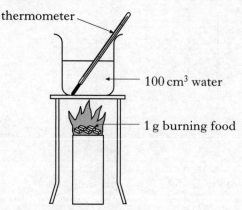

When different foods were burned, the following results were obtained.

Food	Temperature rise (°C)
potato	15
margarine	40
egg	20

The following equation can be used to calculate the energy value of food.

Energy value = 0·42 × temperature rise (°C) (kJ per gram)

Using this equation, the energy value of egg is

A   0·42

B   8·4

C   84

D   840.

20. The energy values of different food groups are shown in the table.

Food group	Energy value (kJ per gram)
Carbohydrate	19
Fat	38
Protein	19

What is the simple whole number ratio of the energy value in fat to protein to carbohydrate?

A   1 : 2 : 1

B   2 : 1 : 1

C   19 : 38 : 19

D   38 : 19 : 19

21. The following statements refer to the state of muscles in the gut.

Statement	State of muscles
1	contracted in front of food
2	relaxed in front of food
3	contracted behind food
4	relaxed behind food

Which statements describe peristalsis?

A   2 and 3

B   1 and 3

C   1 and 4

D   2 and 4

22. Tests were carried out on a sample of food. The result of each test is shown in the table below.

Food test	Iodine solution	Benedict's solution	Biuret solution	Translucent spot
Result	negative	negative	positive	negative

The sample of food contained

A   glucose

B   protein

C   starch

D   fat.

23. Carbon dioxide is removed from the body through the lungs. The correct pathway taken by a molecule of carbon dioxide out of the lungs is

A   alveoli → bronchioles → bronchi → trachea

B   trachea → bronchi → bronchioles → alveoli

C   alveoli → bronchi → bronchioles → trachea

D   trachea → bronchioles → bronchi → alveoli.

24. The graph shows the percentage saturation of haemoglobin at different oxygen concentrations.

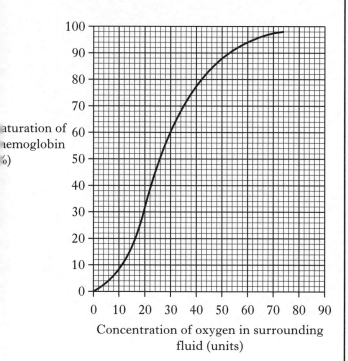

Concentration of oxygen in surrounding fluid (units)

What is the percentage saturation of haemoglobin with oxygen when the oxygen concentration of the surroundings is 60 units?

A 30

B 90

C 92

D 94

25. The diagram below shows a side view of the human brain.

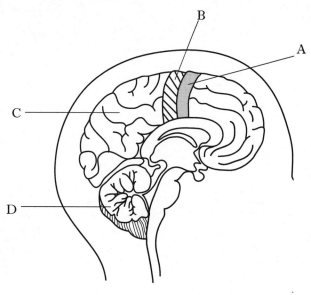

Which label identifies correctly the part of the brain which controls balance?

Candidates are reminded that the answer sheet for Section A MUST be placed INSIDE the front cover of this answer book.

[Turn over

[BLANK PAGE]

SECTION B

All questions in this section should be attempted.
All answers must be written clearly and legibly in ink.

1. (a) *Euglena* is a single celled organism.
   The diagram below shows some of the structures within *Euglena*.

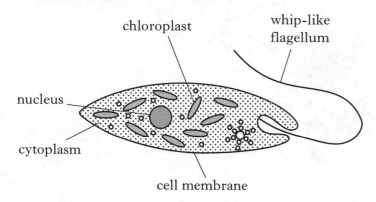

   (i) *Euglena* has structures found in most cells.

   Complete the table below to show the names of these structures and their functions.

Structure	Function
	controls the entry and exit of materials
Cytoplasm	
Nucleus	

   2

   (ii) Name the structure that identifies *Euglena* as a plant cell.

   _____

   1

   (b) Most plant cells have a cell wall.
   Name the structural carbohydrate in the cell wall.

   _____

   1

   [Turn over

Marks

2. Photosynthesis is the process by which green plants make glucose using energy from the sun.

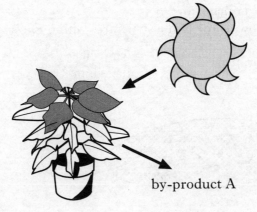

energy from the sun

by-product A

(a) Name the by-product A released during photosynthesis.

_____   1

(b) Hydrogen and a high energy molecule are produced during photolysis.

   (i) Name the high energy molecule.

_____   1

   (ii) Describe the use of hydrogen in carbon fixation.

_____   1

(c)   (i) Explain why an increase in temperature can lead to an increase in the rate of photosynthesis.

_____

_____   2

   (ii) Other than temperature, state **two** limiting factors of photosynthesis.

   1. _____

   2. _____   1

Marks

3. (*a*) The diagram below shows the link between aerobic respiration and protein synthesis.

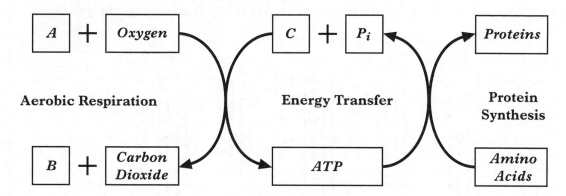

(i) Name substances A, B and C.

A _____

B _____

C _____   2

(ii) Some energy released in respiration can be used for protein synthesis. State one other cellular activity that uses energy.

_____   1

(*b*) The graph below shows lactic acid concentration in blood during a period of vigorous exercise (P) and of complete rest (Q).

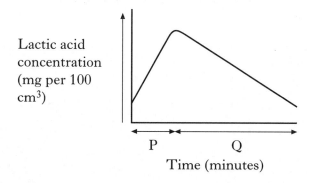

Lactic acid concentration (mg per 100 cm^3)

P   Q

Time (minutes)

Explain why the lactic acid concentration changes during period Q.

_____

_____   1

[Turn over

Marks

4. A student cut five similar cylinders from the same potato, dried them with a paper towel and weighed them.

Each cylinder was placed in a different concentration of sugar solution as shown in the diagram below:

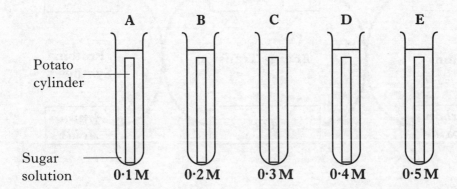

After three hours, the student removed the cylinders from the solutions, dried and weighed them as before.

The results are shown in the table below.

Test tube	Concentration of sugar solution (M)	Initial mass of potato cylinder (g)	Final mass of potato cylinder (g)	Change in mass of potato cylinder (g)	Percentage change in mass of potato
A	0·1	2·0	2·2	+0·2	+10
B	0·2	2·0	2·1	+0·1	+5
C	0·3	2·0	1·8	−0·2	−10
D	0·4	2·0	1·7	−0·3	
E	0·5	2·0	1·5	−0·5	−25

(a) Complete the table by calculating the **percentage change in mass** of the potato cylinder in 0·4 M sugar solution.

Space for calculation

1

(b) (i) Name the variable altered in this investigation.

_____ 1

(ii) Suggest one way in which the reliability of the results could be improved.

_____ 1

Official SQA Past Papers: Intermediate 2 Biology 2008

DO NOT
WRITE IN
THIS
MARGIN

Marks

4. (*b*) (continued)

(iii) Would the results be valid if the cylinders were **not** dried before being weighed? Tick (✓) the correct box.

Valid ☐   Not valid ☐

Explain your answer.

Explanation _____

_____

_____   1

(*c*) (i) State the letter of one test tube containing a potato cylinder in a **hypertonic** solution.

Letter _____   1

(ii) Predict the appearance of the potato cylinder in test tube E after three hours.

_____   1

[Turn over

Marks

5. The pictures show some organisms from a marine ecosystem.

The pictures are not to scale.

sweep   water flea   diatom   euphausid

dinoflagellate   snapper   blenny   pilchard

The table below shows information about the feeding relationships in the marine ecosystem.

Organism	Food eaten
euphasid	dinoflagellate, diatom
dinoflagellate	none
sweep	diatom
snapper	sweep, pilchard, blenny
pilchard	water flea, euphausid
blenny	water flea, euphausid
diatom	none
water flea	diatom, dinoflagellate

(*a*) (i) Use the information in the table to complete the food web below.

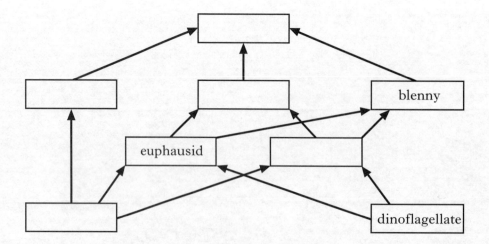

2

(ii) What term is used to describe the snapper in this ecosystem?

_____

1

DO NOT WRITE IN THIS MARGIN

Marks

5. (continued)

(*b*) A pod of dolphins arrived in the area. Dolphins feed on snappers.

Describe the effect of the dolphins on the size of the euphausid population. Explain your answer.

Effect ________________________ **1**

Explanation ____

____ **1**

[Turn over

Marks

6. The table shows the number of pilot whales caught in the Faroe islands between 1994 and 2000.

Year	Number of pilot whales caught
1994	1200
1995	228
1996	1500
1997	1170
1998	820
1999	610
2000	580

(*a*) (i) Construct a **bar graph** of the results given from **1996** to **2000**.

(Additional graph paper, if required, will be found on page 32)

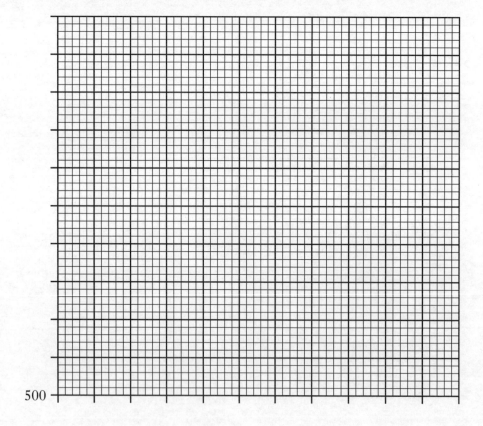

500

3

Marks

6. (*a*) **(continued)**

(ii) Describe the trend shown by the results in the table from **1996** to **2000**.

_____

_____ 1

(iii) What is the average yearly pilot whale catch from **1996** to **2000**?

Space for calculation

average _____ 1

(*b*) How many times greater was the pilot whale catch in 1996 than in 1994?

Space for calculation

_____ times 1

[Turn over

Marks

7. Feather colour in parrots is controlled by a single gene. Blue feather colour (B) is dominant to yellow feather colour (b).

(a) A homozygous blue parrot is crossed with a homozygous yellow parrot.

(i) Complete the genotypes of the P generation.

P   phenotype   blue   X   yellow

P   genotype   _____   _____   1

(ii) State the genotype of the F_1 parrots.

F_1 genotype   _____   1

(iii) State the phenotype of the F_1 parrots.

F_1 phenotype _____   1

(b) An F_1 individual is crossed with a true breeding yellow parrot.

Complete the punnet square to show the expected results of this cross.

Genotype of gametes
from F_1 parent

Genotype of gametes from yellow parent		

2

Marks

8. (*a*) In African grasslands impala, giraffe and zebra feed on *Acacia* trees. Impala and zebra also graze on grasses.

Acacia　　　　　impala　　　　　giraffe　　　　　zebra

(i) State one way that competition for food is reduced between zebras and giraffes.

_____ 1

(ii) The *Acacia* tree is adapted to withstand long periods of drought.

Suggest an adaptation the *Acacia* tree may show that allows it to survive long, dry periods.

_____ 1

(*b*) In Scottish grasslands, sheep are often found as grazers. A very large flock of sheep was introduced into an area of ungrazed grassland.

Explain why this would decrease biodiversity within this area.

_____

_____ 2

[Turn over

DO N
WRIT
TH
MAR

Marks

9. The diagram below shows a section through a human heart.

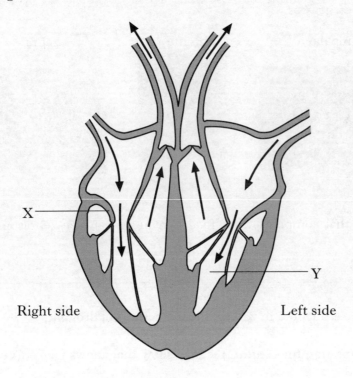

Right side   Left side

(a) Name valve X and chamber Y shown in the diagram.

X _____

Y _____   1

(b) Decide if each of the following statements about blood vessels is **True** or **False**, and tick (✓) the appropriate box.

If the statement is **False**, write the correct word in the **Correction** box to replace the word(s) underlined in the statement.

Statement	True	False	Correction
Capillaries contain valves.			
Veins allow gas exchange.			
Blood leaves the heart in arteries.			

3

Marks

9. (continued)

(*c*) The sentences below describe some of the functions of blood cells.

Underline one option in each set of brackets to make the sentences correct.

Oxygen is transported by $\left\{ \begin{array}{c} \text{red} \\ \text{white} \end{array} \right\}$ blood cells.

It combines with haemoglobin to form oxyhaemoglobin at $\left\{ \begin{array}{c} \text{low} \\ \text{high} \end{array} \right\}$ oxygen levels.

1

Antibodies are produced by $\left\{ \begin{array}{c} \text{macrophages} \\ \text{lymphocytes} \end{array} \right\}$

1

[Turn over

DO NO
WRITE
THIS
MARG

Marks

10. The chart below shows the temperature of a patient over a 5 day period.
Readings were taken daily at 7am and 7pm.

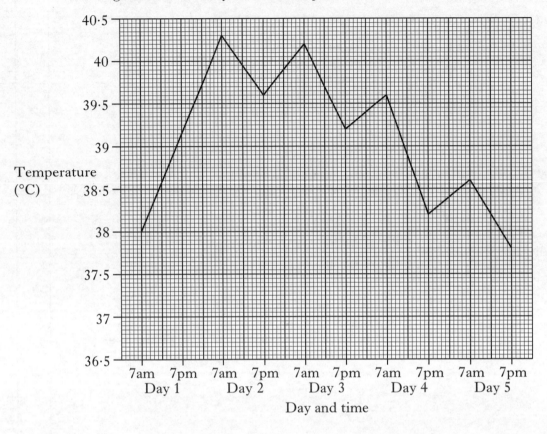

(a)   (i)   Calculate the temperature increase from 7am on Day 1 to 7am on Day 2.

Space for working

_____ °C   **1**

(ii)   State **two** responses made by the body to cause the change in
temperature observed on Day 2 from 7am to 7pm.

1. _____

2. _____   **2**

Marks

10. (continued)

(*b*) (i) Name the area of the brain containing the temperature regulating centre.

_____

1

(ii) What term is used to describe the type of control mechanism which returns the body temperature to normal?

_____

1

(iii) Describe how information is carried from temperature receptors in the skin to the brain.

_____

1

[Turn over

Marks

11. The diagram below shows the human urinary system with its blood supply.

blood flow

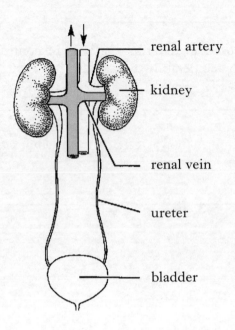

An investigation was carried out to measure the concentration of three substances in samples of blood and urine.

The table below shows the results of this investigation.

Sample site	Concentration (grams per litre)		
	Glucose	Urea	Salts
Renal artery	1·0	0·3	8·0
Renal vein	0·8	0·0	6·0
Ureter	0·0	20·0	15·0

(i) Calculate the percentage of glucose remaining in the blood after it passes through the kidney.

Space for calculation

_____% 1

(ii) Explain how the data in the table supports the statement that urea is a waste product.

_____

_____ 1

(iii) Name one substance, not shown in the table, which is present in urine.

_____ 1

DO NOT WRITE IN THIS MARGIN

Marks

11. (continued)

(*b*) Name the two processes in the kidney which cause the differences in salt concentration between blood and urine.

Process 1 ______________________________ **1**

Process 2 ______________________________ **1**

(*c*) Freshwater bony fish use their kidneys to overcome a water balance problem.

Describe this problem and **one** method used by the kidneys to overcome it.

Problem ______________________________ **1**

Method ______________________________ **1**

[Turn over

Marks

12. (a) The diagram below shows the small intestine with associated organs and blood vessels.

Key: ⟶ direction of flow

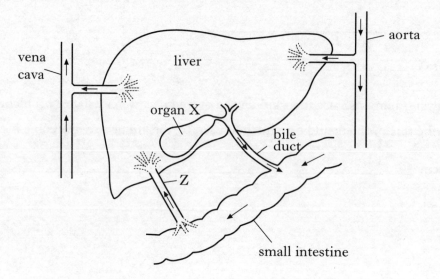

(i) Blood vessel Z carries amino acids to the liver.

  (A) Name blood vessel Z.

  _____   1

  (B) Describe what happens to excess amino acids in the liver.

  _____   1

(ii) (A) Name organ X.

  _____   1

  (B) Describe the function of the bile that is released from organ X.

  _____   1

(b) Complete the table below which shows the substrate and product of two enzymes found in the small intestine.

Enzyme	Substrate	Product
	protein	
amylase		maltose

2

[Turn over for Section C on *page twenty-eight*

Marks

SECTION C

Both questions in this section should be attempted.

Note that each question contains a choice.

**Questions 1 and 2 should be attempted on the blank pages which follow.
All answers must be written clearly and legibly in ink.**

Supplementary sheets, if required, may be obtained from the invigilator.

1. Answer **either** A **or** B.

A. The diagram below shows a section through a flower.

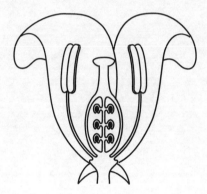

Name the sites of production of pollen grains and ovules in a flower.
Describe how these gametes are formed and describe the process of fertilisation.

5

OR

B. The diagram below summarises a form of genetic engineering.

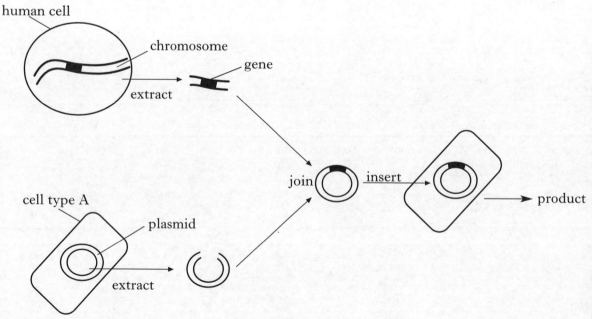

Identify cell type A and name a product of genetic engineering.
Describe the advantages and disadvantages of this process.

5

Question 2 is on *Page thirty*.

SPACE FOR ANSWER TO QUESTION 1

[Turn over for Question 2 on *Page thirty*

Marks

2. Answer **either** A **or** B.

Labelled diagrams may be included where appropriate.

A. Describe the function of yeast in bread making and the anaerobic pathway of respiration involved in this process.　　**5**

OR

B. Describe the properties of enzymes and the function of the enzyme phosphorylase in a synthesis reaction.　　**5**

[END OF QUESTION PAPER]

DO NOT
WRITE IN
THIS
MARGIN

SPACE FOR ANSWER TO QUESTION 2

[Turn over

DO
WRIT
TH
MAR

ADDITIONAL SPACE FOR ANSWERS

ADDITIONAL GRAPH PAPER FOR QUESTION 6(*a*)(i)

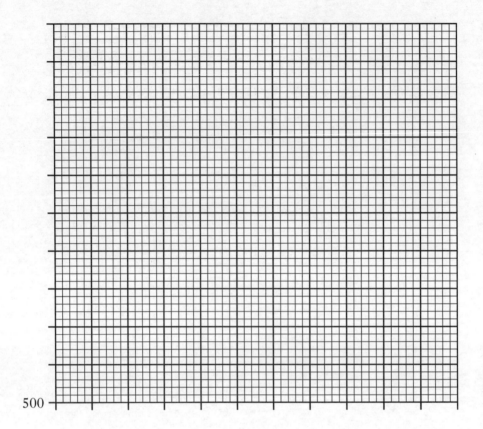

500